MARY BERRY
Cooking for Celebrations

MARY BERRY

Cooking for Celebrations

THAMES MACDONALD

A Thames Macdonald Book

© Thames Macdonald 1986

First published in Great Britain in 1986
by Macdonald & Co (Publishers) Ltd
London & Sydney

A member of BPCC plc

in association with
Thames Television Limited

Reprinted 1986

British Library Cataloguing in Publication Data

Berry, Mary, *1935–*
    Cooking for celebrations.
    1. Entertaining   2. Cookery
    I. Title
    641.5'68   TX731

ISBN 0-356-10747-7

Filmset by Text Filmsetters Limited

Printed and bound in Great Britain by
Purnell Book Production Ltd,
Member of the BPCC Group,
Paulton, Bristol.

Editor: Julie Dufour
Production: John Moulder
Cover Photography: James Jackson
Food Photography: Edmund Goldspink
Stylist: Dawn Lane
Home Economist: Jacki Baxter
Illustrator: Colin Lewis
Contributor: Jill Visser

Macdonald & Co (Publishers) Ltd
Greater London House
Hampstead Road
London   NW1 7QX

Equipment and supplies

Most equipment for making cakes can be bought from ordinary hardware stores or cake shops. However, if you do have a problem getting equipment, the two companies below have very good catalogues and everything, from almond paste to cake tins, can be obtained by mail order.

Mary Ford Cake Artistry Centre Ltd, 28 Southbourne Grove, Bournemouth, BH63 3RA, (0202) 422 653.
Woodnuts Ltd, 97 Church Road, Howe, Sussex, BN3 2BA, (0273) 738840.

For forget-me-not flower cutters, icing smoothers and small stainless steel rolling pins, write to the following address.

Mr & Mrs Craig, *Precision Machining Ltd*, Brember Road, South Harrow, Middlesex.

If you wish to hire equipment, such as china or furniture, or a hall or marquee, check in your local press or consult the Yellow Pages.

It is difficult to know how much drink you will require, but many wine shops and local suppliers will supply on a sale or return basis and lend glasses free of charge. They will, however, expect these to be returned clean and you will have to pay for any breakages.

You can save money by bulk buying, so see if the Cash and Carry in your area allows retail customers – some do. And for fresh goods, such as fruits, vegetables and flowers, try your nearest wholesale market.

Acknowledgements

The publishers would like to thank the following for the loan of props:
Harrods Ltd
Mappin and Webb Ltd
David Mellor

We would also like to thank *Family Circle* magazine for their permission to adapt some illustrations on pages 60-1.

Our special thanks to Jill Visser for contributing the section on doing up a village hall.

CONTENTS

Setting the scene for a wedding or christening party (see page 60)

INTRODUCTION

Family celebration parties are often some of the best and it is lovely to cater for them at home with the help of good friends who are keen cooks and willing to lend a hand. If you are unsure about quantities to serve, there is a guide on page 59, and you will find advice on buying or hiring equipment and where to get your supplies of food and drink at the front of the book.

We have thoroughly enjoyed trying these recipes, although I must confess that some of them haven't been served for the correct occasion. The celebration salmon went down very well at the supper after our annual boys' cricket match. They couldn't believe their eyes, as it's normally pizzas or a barbecue on such occasions.

My special thanks go to Debbie Woolhead, who has lived through the events and occasions of this book with me, trying out all the recipes, and has helped to create all the cakes – the duck and snooker table are her specialities. I have to confess I have only ever made three wedding cakes; my own, a great girlfriend Penny's, and now this peach one. I thoroughly enjoyed an icing course with Mary Ford in Bournemouth. I learned so much in just two days, you can see the results in this book.

SPECIAL OCCASION CAKES

The cake is usually the centrepiece of the festivity. A rich fruit
cake may be made months in advance if it suits you. Cool, wrap
in cling film then foil and store in the freezer. Leave in the
wrapping and thaw slowly for a couple of days in a cool cupboard
before icing. A sponge cake may be made ahead too and frozen in the
same way, although it will thaw quicker. With modern ovens there
is no need to wrap the cake tin for a rich fruit cake in brown paper
because the oven temperature is low enough to let the
cake brown slowly and gently. Although I have given the
recipes for both almond paste and rolled fondant icing, do buy
both if you have a good supplier; local bakers sometimes have
excellent almond paste. Cake boards are often difficult to get for
unusual measurements. You can easily buy offcuts of wood cut
to size at DIY shops – or you may well have wood in the shed and
a handy husband. Just cover the wood or hardboard with foil
and put a thin band of ribbon around the edge.
For a quick pretty decoration,
make a posy of small fresh flowers – freesias, small
rosebuds, sweet peas, gentians, camellias or whatever
you have – secure with ribbons and a Happy
Birthday label and lay on the cake. Arrange the candles around.

Traditional Old English Fruit Cake

Round tin	7 inch 17 cm	8 inch 20 cm	9 inch 22.5 cm	10 inch 25 cm	11 inch 27.5 cm	12 inch 30 cm	13 inch 33 cm
Square tin	6 inch 15 cm	7 inch 17 cm	8 inch 20 cm	9 inch 22.5 cm	10 inch 25 cm	11 inch 27.5 cm	12 inch 30 cm
Mixed dried fruit including peel	8 oz/225 g	1 lb/450 g	1½ lb/675 g	2 lb/1 kg	2½ lb/1.25 kg	3 lb/1.5 kg	3½ lb/1.7 kg
Stoned raisins	2 oz/50 g	4 oz/100 g	6 oz/175 g	8 oz/225 g	10 oz/275 g	12 oz/350 g	14 oz/400 g
Apricot pieces	2 oz/50 g	4 oz/100 g	6 oz/175 g	8 oz/225 g	10 oz/275 g	12 oz/350 g	14 oz/400 g
Glacé cherries	2 oz/50 g	4 oz/100 g	6 oz/175 g	8 oz/225 g	10 oz/275 g	12 oz/350 g	14 oz/400 g
Currants	2 oz/50 g	4 oz/100 g	6 oz/175 g	8 oz/225 g	10 oz/275 g	12 oz/350 g	14 oz/400 g
Inexpensive medium sherry	2½ fl oz/65 ml	¼ pint/150 ml	good ¼ pint 150 ml	½ pint/300 ml	good ½ pint 300 ml	¾ pint/450 ml	good ¾ pint 450 ml
Soft margarine	3 oz/75 g	6 oz/175 g	9 oz/250 g	12 oz/350 g	15 oz/425 g	1 lb 2 oz/500 g	1 lb 5 oz/575 g
Dark muscovado sugar	3 oz/75 g	6 oz/175 g	9 oz/250 g	12 oz/350 g	15 oz/425 g	1 lb 2 oz/575 g	1 lb 5 oz/575 g
Lemons	1	1	2	2	3	3	4
Oranges	1	1	2	2	3	3	4
Eggs size 3	2	3	5	6	7	9	10
Self-raising flour	1 oz/25 g	2 oz/50 g	3 oz/75 g	4 oz/100 g	5 oz/150 g	6 oz/175 g	7 oz/200 g
Plain flour	2 oz/50 g	4 oz/100 g	6 oz/175 g	8 oz/225 g	10 oz/275 g	12 oz/350 g	14 oz/400 g
Blanched almonds	1 oz/25 g	2 oz/50 g	3 oz/75 g	4 oz/100 g	5 oz/150 g	6 oz/175 g	7 oz/200 g
Black treacle	½ level tbsp	1 level tbsp	1½ level tbsp	2 level tbsp	2½ level tbsp	3 level tbsp	3½ level tbsp
Ground mixed spice	½ tsp	1 tsp	1½ tsp	2 tsp	2½ tsp	3 tsp	3½ tsp

Baking time

Round tin	7 inch 17 cm	8 inch 20 cm	9 inch 22·5 cm	10 inch 25 cm	11 inch 27.5 cm	12 inch 30 cm	13 inch 33 cm
Square tin	6 inch 15 cm	7 inch 17 cm	8 inch 20 cm	9 inch 22.5 cm	10 inch 25 cm	11 inch 27.5 cm	12 inch 30 cm
Total baking time	2¾ hrs	3¼ hrs	3½ hrs	3¾ hrs	4¼ hrs	4¾ hrs	5 hrs
at 300°F/150°C/ Gas Mark 2	2 hrs	2 hrs	2 hrs	2 hrs	2 hrs	2 hrs	2 hrs
then at 275°F/140°C/ Gas Mark 1	¾ hr	1¼ hrs	1½ hrs	1¾ hrs	2¼ hrs	2¾ hrs	3 hrs

Quantities of almond paste

round cake	square cake	almond paste
7 inch/17 cm	6 inch/15 cm	1 lb (450 g)
8 inch/20 cm	7 inch/17 cm	1½ lb (675 g)
9 inch/22.5 cm	8 inch/20 cm	1¾ lb (750 g)
10 inch/25 cm	9 inch/22.5 cm	2 lb (900 g)
11 inch/27.5 cm	10 inch/25 cm	2¼ lb (1 kg)
12 inch/30 cm	11 inch/27.5 cm	2½ lb (1.1 kg)
13 inch/33 cm	12 inch/30 cm	3 lb (1.3 kg)

Quantities of rolled fondant icing

round cake	square cake	fondant icing bought	home-made
7 inch/17 cm	6 inch/15 cm	1 lb (450 g)	¾ recipe
8 inch/20 cm	7 inch/17 cm	1½ lb (675 g)	1 × recipe
9 inch/22.5 cm	8 inch/20 cm	1¾ lb (750 g)	1½ × recipe
10 inch/25 cm	9 inch/22.5 cm	2¼ lb (1 kg)	2 × recipe
11 inch/27.5 cm	10 inch/25 cm	2¾ lb (1.2 kg)	2½ × recipe
12 inch/30 cm	11 inch/27.5 cm	3 lb (1.3 kg)	2¾ × recipe
13 inch/33 cm	12 inch/30 cm	3¼ lb (1.4 kg)	3 × recipe

Method for fruit cake

First prepare the fruit. Chop the raisins with a damp knife and quarter the cherries. Put the fruit in a container and pour over the sherry, cover with a lid and leave to soak for at least 3 days, stirring daily.

Put the margarine, sugar, lemon and orange rind and juice, eggs, treacle and chopped almonds in a large bowl. Sift together the flours and spice and add to the bowl. Mix together until evenly blended. Stir in the soaked fruit and sherry.

Heat the oven to 300°F/150°C/gas mark 2 and grease and line the appropriate-size tin with greased greaseproof paper. Spoon the mixture into the tin and smooth the top. Bake in the oven for the time suggested on the chart. If making several tiers for a cake, the best results are obtained by baking the tiers one at a time. To check when the cake is done, pierce through the centre of the cake with a warm skewer. If it comes out clean, then the cake is cooked. If not, cook for a further 15 minutes. If during the cooking time the cake seems to be getting too brown on top, cover it very loosely with a sheet of foil. Leave to cool in the tin.

Basic Recipe for Almond Paste

If you would rather buy ready-prepared almond paste, there are some excellent makes available, such as Mary Ford's (address at the front of the book). This recipe makes about 1½ lb (675 g) of almond paste.

8 oz (225 g) ground almonds
8 oz (225 g) caster sugar
8 oz (225 g) icing sugar, sieved
4 egg yolks, or 2 whole size 3 eggs
about 6 drops almond essence

Mix the dry ingredients together in a bowl, then add the yolks or whole eggs and almond essence. Knead together to form a stiff paste. Try not to overknead the paste as this will make it oily. Store in the refrigerator wrapped in cling film until required.

To cover with almond paste

(See page 11 for quantities.)
1 Brush the cake all over with apricot glaze.
2 Roll out the almond paste onto a table sprinkled with sieved icing sugar, roll out 2 inches (5 cm) larger than the cake.
3 Lift the paste onto a rolling pin, then unroll on top of the cake. Trim off at base.
4 Level the top with a plastic smoother or hand, then smooth the sides. Finish by smoothing with the side of the hand.
5 Transfer the finished cake to silicone or waxed paper.

Bought Rolled Fondant Icing

Having tried various makes, I recommend Renshaws' Regalice, which is available from some bakers and good delicatessens and from Woodnuts (address at the front of the book).

Basic Recipe for Home-made Rolled Fondant Icing

Liquid glucose may be bought from good chemists and keeps on the larder shelf.

about 1 lb 2 oz (500 g) icing sugar
1 generous tablespoon liquid glucose
1 egg white

Sieve the icing sugar into a large mixing bowl, make a well in the centre and add liquid glucose and egg white, knead together until the mixture forms a soft ball. Turn onto a surface sprinkled with sieved icing sugar, knead for about 10 minutes until brilliant white in colour. Keep adding sieved icing sugar if the mixture is a bit sticky. Any colouring can be added at this stage. Store in the refrigerator wrapped in cling film until required.

To cover with rolled fondant icing

(If necessary, this can be done the same day. See page 11 for quantities.)
1 Brush the almond-pasted cake with sherry, rum or kirsch.
2 Roll out the icing 2 inches (5 cm) larger than the cake on a table sprinkled with sieved icing sugar.
3 Lift the icing onto a rolling pin, then unroll on top of the almond paste. Smooth quickly over with your hands. Trim off at base.
4 Smooth the top with the palm of your hand, then the sides. Prick any air bubbles sideways with a pin.
5 To fix the cake on the board, take a piece of icing and dip in alcohol. Place in the centre of the board.
6 Drop the cake onto the board.
7 Smooth carefully.
8 Ideally leave undecorated for 3-4 days to dry, then decorate.

Basic Recipe for Royal Icing

I've used this mainly for piping decoration around the cakes in this section. This could also be made using an electric mixer.

2 egg whites
1 lb 2 oz (500 g) icing sugar, sieved
about 4 teaspoons lemon juice

Put the whites in a large mixing bowl and whisk lightly with a fork until bubbles begin to form on the surface. Add about half the icing sugar and lemon juice and beat well with a wooden spoon for about 10 minutes until really white. Gradually stir in the remaining icing sugar until the correct consistency for piping. This gives sufficient icing to decorate the three tier wedding cake. For single layer cakes, prepare half the quantity of icing.

To make the template for the sugar frills

1 Take a piece of greaseproof paper.
2 Measure the side of the cake and draw accurately on the paper.
3 Divide the diagram of the side of the cake in four vertically and half horizontally.
4 Draw a curved line to mark where the frills should be attached to the cake by joining the points where the division lines have crossed.
5 Cut out the template and use for marking the side of the cake as described in the recipe.

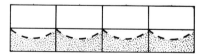

To make sugar frills

1 Colour the paste the day before with peach colouring for frills. Colour one third dark peach, one third light peach and leave the remainder white. Use about 12 oz (350 g) of each colour paste for frills for three tiers. Always finish top frill with the same colour as the cake. With this wedding cake it will be white.

2 Make templates from greaseproof paper for each cake.

3 Pin the template onto the cake, then mark out with a hat pin or cocktail stick.

4 Cut out the thinly rolled paste into circles using a 3½ inch (8 cm) pastry cutter and cut out the middle with a plain 1½ inch (4 cm) cutter.

5 Roll the fluted edge with a cocktail stick; going over several flutes, roll firmly backwards and forwards. Dust the table with icing sugar, and dust the cocktail stick to prevent it from sticking. A large cake will take four half circles on each side.

6 To attach circles to rolled fondant icing, stick on with water along marked lines, after removing the template. Attach three layers of frills, starting with dark peach, then light peach and finishing with white, to the sides of the cakes.

7 Using a number 2 plain piping nozzle, pipe a line of small dots along the line where the frill is joined to the cake. Make ribbon decorations and roses (see page 14). Fix into a sausage of fondant on the cake.

To decorate with piping

1 Pipe a line of shells around the edge of the cake.

2 Using a plain nozzle, outline the edge of the shells as shown above.

3 Overpipe with dark coloured icing using a plain writing nozzle.

To make ribbon loop sprays

To make loop sprays, loop pieces of ribbon and secure with fine florists wire. Cut lengths of ribbon as tailpieces and attach separately.

Crescent spray

I used white and peach ribbon for this for the wedding cake. Make four loops in white ribbon and four in peach, put together alternately to form a crescent spray and secure in the centre with florists' wire. Cut two lengths each of peach and white ribbon as tailpieces and attach two tailpieces either side of the spray. Stick onto the cake with a small piece of icing.

Forget-me-not Cut-out Sugar Flowers

These little forget-me-not type flowers are so easy to make and are done with a spring flower cutter and white covered wire, all available from the addresses at the front of the book.

rolled fondant icing, coloured blue
white covered wire
a little cornflour
yellow glacé icing
piping bag fitted with number 2 nozzle
small flower cutter

Cut the wire into 3 inch (7.5 cm) lengths, make a small hook in the top of each length. For each flower, roll out a little of the paste on a surface sprinkled with cornflour. Using a small flower cutter, stamp out a flower, push the wire through the centre of the flower, so that the hooked end of the wire forms the middle of the flower. Pipe a little of the yellow icing in the middle of the flower to secure the wire, push the petals up gently to give the flower more depth and make it look more lifelike. Lay on a cooling rack to dry out.

These flowers look pretty in a bunch on top of a cake (see the anniversary cake, page 16). Cut-out flowers without the wire can be used with a little piped icing to decorate a cake or be secured to the bow on the side of the cake (see the golden wedding cake, page 16).

Crystallized Fresh Garden Flowers

Choose flowers that have a good strength of colour. I have had success with the following.

red japonica
hyacinths, broken carefully into
  separate bells
primroses
small roses such as garnette or fairy
  roses
dog roses, the darker the better
cultivated violets
aubretia, individual flower heads
freesias
Christmas roses

Lightly beat an egg white, brush all over the flower on all sides, then sprinkle with caster sugar. Either stand on a wire cooling tray or lay on silicone paper. Leave overnight to dry out in a warm place. Leaves can also be crystallized. Once dry, arrange on the cake with a little icing. Most flowers stay looking good for up to 2 weeks.

To make moulded roses

1 Make a cone shape. Take a piece of paste and roll to the size of a large pea with the hands.
2 Put a ball of paste between two pieces of polythene – a split bag will do – and flatten out to the shape of a petal and using your thumb make it very thin at the edges. Mould the first petal around the cone fairly lightly. Take another ball and make another petal. Place it opposite the join of the first petal. Press the left-hand edge in firmly and leave the right side of the petal open. Make another petal and tuck in the left side and leave the right open. Pinch the edge to soften.
3 Continue for about 5 petals, pinch in the base, then add about 6 further petals.
4 Gently break off the rose from the cone and re-form the rose gently. Leave to become firm overnight.

Wedding Cake

one 8 inch (20 cm) square fruit
  cake
one 10 inch (25 cm) square fruit
  cake
one 12 inch (30 cm) square fruit
  cake
7 lb (3.2 kg) almond paste
7¾ lb (3.3 kg) bought or 7 ×
  recipe for rolled fondant icing
  (see page 12)
3 square cake boards, one 10 inch
  (25 cm), one 12 inch (30 cm) and
  one 14 inch (35 cm)
8 pillars with holes in the middle for
  dowelling
wooden dowelling, about 54 inches
  (135 cm), for the pillars
sugar frills to go round cake (see
  page 13)
1 × recipe for royal icing (see
  page 12)
sugar roses and ribbons to decorate

To assemble the cake, cover the cakes with almond paste and rolled fondant icing as suggested in the step-by-step instructions, prepare the sugar frills and secure to the sides of the cakes. Pipe a fine line of shells around the bottom of each cake. Prepare the roses and bows (see page 13) and arrange on the tops of the cakes, choose coloured ribbons to match the frills on the outside of the cake.

Mark lightly on the cakes where the pillars will stand. Sink wooden dowelling into the cakes, measure and withdraw, then cut to size. Place in position on the cakes and stand the pillars on top. The wooden dowelling supports the weight of the cakes and prevents the top layers from sinking into the bottom layers.

Snooker Table

If you can knit, then knit a few pockets to go round the table – it really does look authentic.

For the cake
6 oz (175 g) soft margarine
3 eggs
8 oz (225 g) self-raising flour
1½ level teaspoons baking powder
6 oz (175 g) caster sugar
3 tablespoons milk

To fill and decorate
strawberry jam
4 oz (100 g) butter, softened
8 oz (225 g) icing sugar, sieved
1¼ lb (550 g) bought or 1 × recipe
    for rolled fondant icing, coloured
    green (see page 12)
coloured sweets for snooker balls
1 × recipe for royal icing, half
    coloured brown (see page 12)
wooden dowelling for cues

Heat the oven to 350°F/180°C/gas mark 4 and then grease and line with greased greaseproof paper a roasting tin of about about 12 × 9 inches (30 × 22.5 cm).

Put the margarine, eggs, flour, baking powder, sugar and milk in a bowl and beat well for about 2 minutes until well blended. Turn the mixture into the tin and smooth the top. Bake in the oven for about 40 minutes until the cake has shrunk from the sides of the tin and springs back when lightly pressed with a finger. Leave to cool in the tin, then turn out and peel off the paper.

Divide the cake in three and sandwich together with jam. Mix the butter and icing sugar together until thoroughly blended and spread over the cake. Roll out the icing and use to cover the cake. Pipe bold lines of brown icing around the sides of the cake to form the outside of the table.

Pipe the markings on the table in white icing with a fine number 2 nozzle. Use a little icing to secure the balls on the table and lay the cues on the cake. If you have been clever enough to knit little pockets, secure these with pins to the sides of the cake.

Snooker Table

Heart-shaped Anniversary Cake

Golden Wedding Cake

Heart-shaped Anniversary Cake

To make one 10 inch (25 cm) heart-shaped fruit cake, use the quantity for a 10 inch (25 cm) round cake. The shape of the cake tin means that it needs a longer cooking time, so do test for doneness with a fine skewer before taking it out of the oven.

one 10 inch (25 cm) heart-shaped
    fruit cake
2¼ lb (1 kg) almond paste
2¾ lb (1.2 kg) bought or 2½ ×
    recipe for rolled fondant icing
    (see page 12)
cake board
lace to go round bottom of cake
bunch of cut-out sugar flowers
ribbon to go round flowers

Assemble the cake as suggested in the step-by-step instructions, covering it with almond paste and fondant icing. Decorate with lace and flowers. For a more personal note, you could pipe the names of the couple on the cake, but one of the joys of this cake is that there is no piping involved.

Golden Wedding Cake

This cake is also perfect for an 18th or 21st birthday. Just add your own writing and change the colours to suit the occasion.

one 10 inch (25 cm) round fruit
    cake
apricot glaze
2 lb (900 g) almond paste
2¼ lb (1 kg) bought or 2 × recipe
    for rolled fondant icing, coloured
    gold (see page 12)
½ recipe for royal icing (see
    page 12)
food colouring
gold ribbon to go round the cake
a few cut-out sugar flowers
one 12 inch (30 cm) cake board
crystallized daisy chrysanthemums,
    freesias or primroses

See notes on covering with almond paste and rolled fondant icing to assemble the cake on the board. Pipe royal icing around the bottom of the cake following the step-by-step instructions (see page 13). Pipe the wording on the top of the cake with a number 2 plain icing nozzle. Tie the ribbon round the cake and put on a big bow. It is easiest to tie the bow separately and then secure it onto the side of the cake with a pin. Decorate with a few cut-out sugar flowers. Decorate the cake with crystallized or fresh flowers just before serving it. With this cake, remember to keep the piping to a minimum; it is so easy to spoil the effect of the flowers by adding too much piping.

Christening Cake

Use any of the suggested flowers according to the season. My most successful cake was with red japonica, which grows up the side of the house. Alternatively, decorate with fresh or silk flowers, or crystallized dog roses.

one 10 inch (25 cm) round fruit
    cake
2¼ lb (1 kg) almond paste
2¼ lb (1 kg) bought or 2 × recipe
    for rolled fondant icing (see
    page 12)
½ recipe for royal icing (see
    page 12)
12 inch (30 cm) round cake board
ribbon to go round the cake
crystallized dog roses or artificial
    silk flowers to decorate

Assemble the cake on the board by following the step-by-step instructions for covering with almond paste and fondant icing. Pipe shells around the bottom of the cake and with a number 2 plain icing nozzle pipe the child's name on the top of the cake. Secure the ribbon and the bow on the side of the cake and decorate with crystallized flowers.

Christening Cake

Yellow Duck Cake

This is a favourite with the very young. Remember you can always make your own cake board by covering a suitably-sized piece of chip board with foil.

For the cake
8 oz (225 g) soft margarine
8 oz (225 g) caster sugar
4 large eggs, beaten
8 oz (225 g) self-raising flour
2 level teaspoons baking powder

To fill and decorate
strawberry jam
4 oz (100 g) butter, softened
8 oz (225 g) icing sugar, sieved
2¼ lb (1 kg) bought or 2 × recipe
   for rolled fondant icing (see
   page 12)
yellow and orange food colouring
green ribbon
cake board

Heat the oven to 350°F/180°C/gas mark 4. Grease and line with greased greaseproof paper a 5 inch (12.5 cm) and a 10 inch (25 cm) round cake tin.

Put the margarine, sugar, eggs, flour and baking powder in a large bowl and beat well for about 2 minutes until smooth and blended. Divide between the tins, using about a quarter of the mixture for the small tin. Bake in the oven until golden brown and the cakes spring back when lightly pressed with a finger. The small cake will take about 20 minutes and the larger cake about 40 minutes. Turn the cakes out onto a wire rack to cool, removing the paper.

Divide each cake in half and sandwich together with jam. From the large cake cut out the shapes required for the body of the duck (see illustration below); the small cake forms the head. Mix the butter and icing sugar together and spread around each piece of cake. Leave a small piece of icing white, colour the remainder yellow and use to cover the body,

head and tail, covering each piece separately. Colour what is left of the yellow icing orange and use to cover the feet and beak. Arrange the pieces together on a board. Make the duck's eye from the white icing with a blob of orange icing in the middle and secure a large bow around its neck.

Birthday Party Cake

This is very popular with the girls; they love to see their names up in lights.

For the cake
8 oz (225 g) soft margarine
8 oz (225 g) caster sugar
4 large eggs, beaten
8 oz (225 g) self-raising flour
2 level teaspoons baking powder

To fill and decorate
strawberry jam
3 oz (75 g) butter, softened
6 oz (175 g) icing sugar, sieved
2¼ lb (1 kg) bought or 2 × recipe
   for rolled fondant icing (see
   page 12)
food colouring
½ recipe for royal icing (see
   page 12)
ribbon to go round the cake
cake board

Heat the oven to 350°F/180°C/gas mark 4. Grease and line with greased greaseproof paper a 10 inch (25 cm) round cake tin.

Put all the ingredients for the cake in a bowl and beat well for about 2 minutes until blended. Turn into the

tin and bake in the oven for about 50 minutes until golden brown and the centre springs back when lightly pressed with a finger. Turn out onto a wire rack to cool, removing the paper.

Divide the cake in three and sandwich together with jam. Prepare the butter icing by mixing the butter with the icing sugar, then spread over the cake. Cover with rolled fondant icing of whatever colour you choose. Pipe divisions on top of the cake with royal icing and write each child's name in a division. Pipe shells around the bottom of the cake. Secure a ribbon and bow around the cake with a pin. Place a candle in a holder between each division of the cake.

FINGER FOOD AND CANAPÉS

These foods can all be eaten in the hand while standing up.
This seems the most popular sort of buffet for these occasions
in the afternoon, accompanied usually by Champagne or sparkling wine
followed by tea. All the food items should be beautifully prepared and
decorated and be a little larger than drinks party food. The savoury
food often looks good arranged on trays so that, as they are
handed around, the guests can see at a glance what the choice is.
Keep the food in neat rows, or just one kind of savoury
on a plate. Have napkins handy in case the guests'
hands get sticky. If space allows, have a few small tables
and chairs around the edge of the room so older guests
— and weary young ones — can get off their feet.

Salmon Roll-ups

These are a delicious savoury to hand round at parties.

1 uncut firm brown loaf

For the pâté
8 oz (225 g) smoked salmon pieces
5 oz (150 g) butter, melted
4 oz (100 g) rich cream cheese
2 tablespoons tomato purée
juice of ½ lemon
ground black pepper

Put all the ingredients for the pâté in a blender or processor and mix to a smooth paste. If using a blender, it helps to do this in two batches. Taste and check seasoning. Transfer the pâté to a bowl. Cut the crusts off the loaf, then carefully slice the loaf into ⅛ inch (3 mm) slices, lengthwise along the loaf. Generously spread the pâté on the slices of bread, and roll up like a swiss roll. Cut each roll-up into about 16 slices and arrange on a serving dish, garnished with parsley.

Makes about 100 roll-ups

Asparagus Rolls

1 lb (450 g) frozen asparagus, thawed
1 small firm brown loaf
4 oz (100 g) butter, softened

Cook the asparagus for 1 minute in a pan of boiling water, rinse under running cold water, then drain well on kitchen paper. Cut the crusts off the loaf leaving the loaf 2½ inches (6 cm) square and slice thinly; you should be able to get 36 slices from the loaf. Butter the slices of bread, arrange the asparagus across the slices of bread from corner to corner and roll up so that there is a v-shape on the top of the roll. Store in the refrigerator covered with cling film.

Makes 36 rolls

Salmon Roll-ups and Asparagus Rolls

Baby Prawn Quiches

These are best served warm, so make them ahead and reheat just before serving. They take time to prepare but are well worth it.

For the pastry
8 oz (225 g) plain flour
2 oz (50 g) hard margarine
2 oz (50 g) lard
3-4 tablespoons cold water

For the filling
1 oz (25 g) butter
1 small onion, finely chopped
6 oz (175 g) cream cheese
2 eggs, beaten
¼ pint (150 ml) single cream
2 tablespoons lemon juice
salt
freshly ground black pepper
1 tablespoon chopped parsley
6 oz (175 g) peeled prawns

Heat the oven to 375°F/190°C/gas mark 5. Make the pastry in the usual way (see Spinach, Cheese and Bacon Quiche, page 28). Roll out the dough on a lightly floured surface and cut out 20 circles large enough to line deep patty tins. Press the circles into the tins, chill in the refrigerator for about 10 minutes, then line them with foil. Bake in the oven for about 20 minutes, removing the foil for the last 10 minutes to allow the bases to dry out.

Reduce the oven to 325°F/160°C/gas mark 3. Melt the butter in a pan and fry the onion for about 3 minutes until beginning to soften, transfer the onion to a bowl and bind with the cream cheese using a wooden spoon. Gradually add the eggs, then beat in the cream, lemon juice, salt, pepper and parsley until smooth. Divide the prawns between the pastry cases and spoon the egg and cream mixture into the cases. Cook in the oven for about 20 minutes until the filling has set. Arrange on an oven-proof serving dish ready to reheat when required.

Makes about 20 quiches

Asparagus and Gruyère Quiches

Make sure that the pastry is really cooked through on the bottom of the quiche, otherwise it tends to be rather soggy and heavy.

For the pastry
8 oz (225 g) plain flour
2 oz (50 g) hard margarine
2 oz (50 g) lard
about 4 tablespoons cold water

For the filling
4 oz (100 g) Gruyère cheese
8 oz (225 g) can asparagus cocktail spears, drained and chopped
2 eggs, beaten
¼ pint (150 ml) single cream
salt
freshly ground black pepper

Prepare and bake blind the pastry cases (see Baby Prawn Quiches opposite) at 375°F/190°C/gas mark 5.

Reduce the oven to 325°F/160°C/gas mark 3. Arrange slithers of Gruyère cheese in the bottom of each pastry case and divide the asparagus between the quiches. Blend together the eggs, cream and seasoning, then spoon this mixture into the cases. Bake in the oven for about 20 minutes until the filling has set. Arrange on an ovenproof dish ready to reheat when required.

Makes about 20 quiches

Baby Cheese Eclairs

To ensure that the pastry stays nice and crisp, don't fill too far ahead.

Choux pastry
2 oz (50 g) butter
¼ pint (150 ml) water
2½ oz (62.5 g) plain flour
2 eggs, beaten

For the filling
1 oz (25 g) butter
1 oz (25 g) flour
½ pint (300 ml) milk
salt
freshly ground black pepper
1 teaspoon Dijon mustard
a little grated nutmeg
4 oz (100 g) well-flavoured, dry Cheddar cheese, grated

Heat the oven to 425°F/220°C/gas mark 7. Lightly grease a baking sheet.

To make the eclairs, put the butter and water in a pan, slowly bring to the boil and allow the butter to melt. Remove from the heat, add the flour all at once and beat until it forms a soft ball. Gradually beat in the eggs a little at a time to make a smooth shiny paste. Put the mixture in a piping bag fitted with a ½ inch (1.25 cm) plain nozzle and pipe 20 small eclairs on the baking sheet.

Bake in the oven for 10 minutes, then reduce the heat to 375°F/190°C/gas mark 5 and cook for a further 20 minutes until well risen and golden brown. Remove from the oven and split one side of each eclair to allow the steam to escape. Cool on a wire rack.

For the filling, melt the butter in a pan, stir in the flour and cook for a minute. Gradually blend in the milk and bring to the boil, stirring until thickened. Remove from the heat and stir in salt, pepper, mustard, nutmeg and cheese. Allow to cool, then divide the sauce between the eclairs.

Makes about 20 eclairs

Avocado Dip

Serve this dip with a mixture of fresh salad vegetables such as celery sticks, radishes, carrot sticks and cauliflower florets.

2 avocado pears
juice of 1 large lemon
1 tablespoon sunflower oil
1 teaspoon made English mustard
1 teaspoon caster sugar
salt
freshly ground black pepper
¼ pint (150 ml) double cream

Cut the avocado pears in half and remove the stones. Scoop out the flesh and put it in a bowl. Mash well with a fork. Mix the lemon juice, oil, mustard, sugar, salt and pepper together and stir into the mashed avocado. Whisk the cream until it is thick and forms soft peaks. Fold into the avocado mixture. Alternatively, process all the ingredients in a blender or processor until smooth. Turn into a small bowl, place in the centre of a plate and surround with crisp salad vegetables.

Serves 6

Red House Spiced Dip

This is so simple to make and yet quite delicious with drinks.

4 tablespoons mango chutney sauce
2 teaspoons Dijon mustard
1 teaspoon curry powder
8 oz (225 g) rich cream cheese

Put all the ingredients in a bowl and mix well until thoroughly blended. Turn into a bowl or half a fresh pineapple shell and serve with potato crisps, sticks of carrot and celery, and florets of cauliflower.

Serves 6

Pork Sausage, Sage and Onion Rolls, Avocado Dip (see page 21), Red House Dip (see page 21), and Blue Cheese Dip with fresh vegetable sticks, and Flaky Cheese Crackers

Blue Cheese Dip

Serve this refreshing dip, which is perfect to accompany drinks, with a variety of fresh vegetables.

8 oz (225 g) Stilton, crumbled
¼ pint (150 ml) soured cream
¼ pint (150 ml) good mayonnaise

Put all the ingredients in a bowl and mix well until thoroughly blended. Chill well in the refrigerator before serving. Turn into a small bowl, place in the centre of a plate and surround with salad vegetables.

Serves 10

Pork Sausage, Sage and Onion Rolls

A bit of a mouthful to say but it explains what goes in them. If possible, serve them hot, but not too hot to handle. Strong flour is best for the pastry but is not essential.

For the pastry
8 oz (225 g) strong plain flour
6 oz (175 g) hard margarine, very
    well chilled
about ¼ pint (150 ml) water

For the filling
1 oz (25 g) butter
6 oz (175 g) onions, chopped
1 lb (450 g) pork sausagemeat
2 oz (50 g) fresh white breadcrumbs
1 teaspoon dried sage
salt
freshly ground black pepper
a little beaten egg to glaze
watercress to garnish

Measure the flour into a large mixing bowl. Grate the margarine into the flour, using a coarse grater – sprinkle some of the flour over the margarine as it is being grated as this keeps it from sticking. Add the water and mix to a dough with a knife.

Flour a table or a board, roll out the pastry to an oblong and fold in three as if you were making flaky pastry. Wrap in cling film and chill for 15 minutes or so. Roll out and repeat the process three more times. Chill in the refrigerator until required.

For the filling, heat the butter in a pan and quickly fry the onions for about 5 minutes until beginning to soften, then turn into a large mixing bowl. Add the remaining ingredients, season well and mix together until thoroughly blended.

Roll out the prepared pastry to an oblong 12 × 16 inches (30 × 40 cm). Divide lengthwise into three equal strips. Lay 'sausages' of the filling down the centre of each strip. Dampen one long edge with water, wrap over the pastry to seal in the sausagemeat. Divide each strip into 12 small sausage rolls. Arrange close together on a large baking sheet, glaze with beaten egg. Cook in the oven at 400°F/200°C/gas mark 6, for about 25 minutes until well risen and golden brown. Serve warm on a plate garnished with watercress.

Makes about 36 rolls

Flaky Cheese Crackers

These are wonderful for a party. They take time to make but are really well worth it. You can freeze the raw cheese pastry for up to a month, then just slice the crackers from the pastry block and bake them. They are best served warm. Bake these biscuits on silicone paper in batches so you can keep re-using the paper.

1 lb (450 g) strong plain flour
1 good teaspoon salt
1 teaspoon dry mustard
12 oz (350 g) hard margarine, chilled
about ½ pint (300 ml) cold water
8 oz (225 g) well-flavoured, dry Cheddar cheese, grated
2 oz (50 g) Parmesan cheese, grated

Measure the flour, salt and mustard into a large bowl. Grate the margarine into the flour, using a coarse grater; sprinkle some of the flour over the margarine as it is being grated – this keeps it from sticking. Add the cold water and mix to a dough with a knife.

Flour the table, roll out the pastry to an oblong. Divide the mixed grated cheeses into four piles. Sprinkle one-quarter of the cheese over two-thirds of the pastry, fold twice as if you were making flaky pastry, wrap in cling film and chill for 15 minutes or so. Roll out and repeat the process three more times. Wrap and chill overnight or for several hours. If time is short, freeze for at least 2 hours.

Take the block of cheese pastry and cut into ⅛ inch (3 mm) slices through the pastry. Lay these strips flat so that you can see the flaky layers. Cut the strips into 1½ inch (4 cm) pieces. Spread out on baking sheets lined with silicone paper. Bake in the oven at 425°F/220°C/gas mark 7 for about 10 minutes until golden brown and crisp.

Makes about 100 crackers

Ascot Kebabs

These small kebabs are ideal to serve with drinks. Remember to use wooden cocktail sticks; plastic ones would melt when heated.

8 oz (225 g) streaky bacon
15 oz (425 g) can stoned prunes, drained
2 oz (50 g) butter
8 oz (225 g) button mushrooms

Wrap pieces of bacon around each prune and secure with a wooden cocktail stick. Grill under a hot grill until the bacon is cooked and beginning to crisp. Heat the butter in a pan and quickly fry the mushrooms for about 3 minutes. Allow to cool, then secure a mushroom on each side of the bacon roll on the wooden cocktail

sticks. When required, reheat under the grill until warmed through and serve arranged on a warm dish.

Serves 20 with drinks

Baby Meringues

Always use egg whites that are at room temperature and follow the method exactly.

4 egg whites
8 oz (225 g) caster sugar
whipping cream to serve

Heat the oven to 225°F/110°C/gas mark ¼. Line two baking sheets with silicone paper.

Place the egg whites in a large bowl and whisk on high speed with an electric whisk until they form soft peaks. Add the sugar a teaspoonful at a time, whisking well after each addition, until all the sugar has been added. Put the mixture in a piping bag fitted with a ½ inch (1.25 cm) plain icing nozzle and pipe about 50 small blobs on the baking trays. Bake in the oven for about 3-4 hours until the meringues are firm and dry and will lift easily from the silicone paper.

Whisk the cream until thick and use to sandwich the merginue shells together. Serve piled high on a plate.

Makes 25 double meringues

Mini Chocolate Eclairs

These are always a great favourite at parties.

Choux pastry
4 oz (100 g) butter
½ pint (300 ml) water
5 oz (125 g) plain flour
4 eggs, beaten

Filling
1 pint (600 ml) whipping cream,
  whipped

Icing
4 oz (100 g) plain chocolate
4 tablespoons water
1 oz (25 g) butter
6 oz (175 g) icing sugar, sieved

Heat the oven to 425°F/220°C/gas mark 7. Grease two baking sheets.

For the pastry, put the butter and water in a pan, bring to the boil slowly and allow the butter to melt. Remove from the heat, add the flour all at once and beat until it forms a soft ball. Gradually add the eggs a little at a time, beating well to give a smooth shiny paste. Put the mixture into a piping bag fitted with a ½ inch (1.25 cm) plain nozzle and pipe 40 eclairs on the baking sheet. Bake in the oven for 10 minutes, then reduce the temperature to 375°F/190°C/gas mark 5 and cook for a further 15-20 minutes until well risen and golden brown. Remove from the oven and split one side of each eclair to allow steam to escape. When cool, fill each eclair with whipped cream.

For the icing, put the chocolate, water and butter in a bowl and heat gently over a pan of simmering water until the mixture has melted. Remove from the heat and beat in the icing sugar until smooth. Pour the chocolate sauce into a shallow dish and dip each eclair into the sauce to coat the top. Allow to set. Serve arranged on a plate.

Makes about 40 small eclairs

Fresh Fruit Boats

These boats are a bit fiddly to prepare but the end result is well worth it. If you haven't got many boat moulds, cook the boats in batches until all the pastry is used up.

For the cases
8 oz (225 g) plain flour
3 oz (75 g) lard
3 oz (75 g) butter
1 oz (25 g) caster sugar
1 egg yolk
about 2 tablespoons water

For the filling
about 4 tablespoons redcurrant jelly
1 lb (450 g) small whole fresh
  strawberries

Heat the oven to 425°F/220°C/gas mark 7. Put the flour in a bowl and rub in the fats until the mixture resembles fine breadcrumbs. Stir in the sugar, then bind together with the egg yolk and water to give a firm dough. Turn out onto a lightly floured surface, knead lightly, roll out and use to line as many boat moulds as you have. Line with a small piece of foil and bake in the oven on a baking tray for about 12 minutes, removing the foil for the last 5 minutes of cooking time until the pastry is a golden brown. Allow to cool, then lift out of the moulds onto a cooling rack. Repeat until all the pastry has been used.

For the filling, gently heat the jelly in a pan so that it becomes liquid and brush a little on the inside of each boat. Place the strawberries in the boats and spoon over the remaining redcurrant glaze. Arrange on a serving plate and serve with cream.

Makes about 20 boats

Apricot and Almond Boats

20 pastry boats (as above)
4 oz (100 g) almond paste
14 oz (397 g) can apricot halves,
  drained
about 4 tablespoons apricot jam

Prepare the pastry boats as above, arrange a slither of almond paste in the bottom of each boat. Slice the apricots and arrange on top of the almond filling, then glaze with a little apricot jam which has been heated so that it can be brushed over the apricots.

Makes about 20 boats

Almond Biscuits

These biscuits are based on a shortbread mixture and really are quite delicious.

8 oz (225 g) soft margarine, slightly
  warmed
4 oz (100 g) semolina
7 oz (200 g) self-raising flour
4 oz (100 g) caster sugar
about 40 blanched almonds, halved

Heat the oven to 350°F/180°C/gas mark 4. Put all the ingredients, except the nuts, in a bowl and work together until blended with a wooden spoon. You can do this in a processor. Take a large piping bag fitted with a ½ inch (1.25 cm) plain icing nozzle. Pipe about 80 small blobs on two large, greased baking trays. Press a nut in the centre of each. Bake in the oven for 15-20 minutes until a pale golden brown. Cool on a wire rack. Serve attractively arranged on a plate.

Makes about 80 biscuits

TRADITIONAL COLD BUFFET

Choose from these ideas recipes that suit the occasion. Decorate the
table so that it looks beautiful and plan it carefully. If guests
are approaching from the left, the plates, cutlery and napkins should
be the first thing they pick up so that they can help themselves to
the spread. The meats or fish and appropriate sauces are usually laid
out next, followed by the salads and, lastly, the French bread or
rolls. When everything is collected, a glass of wine can be served. It is
a good idea to start carving any meat beforehand, then
to carve the remainder in front of the guests. Delegate
this job to someone you know is good at it and remember a
really sharp knife and carving fork.
The puddings will ideally be on another table, and the cheese
and coffee could perhaps be put back on the buffet
table once it has been cleared of the main course.

Cold Rib of Beef

This is ideal to serve at a party buffet. Order the joint well in advance from your butcher and ask him to almost saw off the vertebrae but leave them attached and to remove the gristle which runs in a long line underneath.

1 fore rib of beef, about 8 lb (3.5 kg)
salt

Heat the oven to 400°F/200°C/gas mark 6.

Rub a little salt over the fat on the beef and stand the ribs upright in a roasting tin. Roast in the oven for 12 minutes per pound (450 g) if you like beef pink in the centre but not dripping blood, or 14 minutes to the pound (450 g) if you like it well done. Remove the meat from the oven and allow it to become quite cold. Chill really well for easier carving.

Serves about 20 or more if served with other meats as part of a buffet

Mild Spiced Chicken Mayonnaise

Ideally make this the day before it is needed so the chicken absorbs the spicy mayonnaise flavour. You could use turkey if preferred.

2½ lb (1.25 kg) cooked
   chicken, chopped
1 medium onion, chopped
1 clove garlic, crushed
2 tablespoons tomato purée
1 level teaspoon curry powder
1 level teaspoon ground turmeric
2 tablespoons lemon juice
4 tablespoons apricot jam
1 pint (600 ml) good
   mayonnaise
salt
freshly ground black pepper
lemon wedges and small sprigs of
   watercress to decorate

Put the onion, garlic, tomato purée, curry powder, ground turmeric, lemon juice and apricot jam in a saucepan and bring to the boil, then simmer gently for a few moments. Reduce to a purée in a processor or blender. Blend with the mayonnaise in a bowl and stir in the chicken and seasoning. Chill overnight in the refrigerator.

Taste and check seasoning. Pile into a serving dish and decorate with lemon wedges and watercress.

Serves 10

Avocado Mousse with Prawns and Sauce Marie Rose

This quantity makes about 4 pints (2.4 litres), so you can either use two 2 pint (1.2 litre) ring moulds or any other shape you like to hold the mixture.

4 avocado pears
1 oz (25 g) powdered gelatine
8 tablespoons cold water
½ pint (300 ml) boiling water
2 chicken stock cubes
2 level teaspoons salt
freshly ground black pepper
a piece of onion the size of a walnut,
   pressed through a garlic press
2 tablespoons lemon juice
1 pint (600 ml) mayonnaise
½ pint (300 ml) double cream,
   lightly whipped
a few prawns for decoration

Sauce
8 oz (225 g) frozen prawns, thawed
½ pint (300 ml) French dressing
½ pint (300 ml) good mayonnaise
2 teaspoons horseradish sauce
2 teaspoons tomato purée
a pinch of caster sugar
salt
freshly ground black pepper

Put the gelatine in a bowl with the cold water. Stand for about 3 minutes to form a sponge, then put the bowl in a pan of simmering water and allow the gelatine to dissolve. Stir the boiling water and stock cubes together until the cubes have dissolved, then stir in the gelatine. Peel and quarter the avocados, remove the stones and crush the flesh with a fork or potato masher. Stir in the stock, salt, pepper, onion and lemon juice. This may be done in a food processor. Leave to cool before folding in the mayonnaise and cream. Divide between two 2 pint (1.2 litre) ring moulds and leave in the refrigerator to set. Turn out and decorate with prawns.

To make the sauce, thoroughly drain the prawns on kitchen paper. Combine with the other ingredients and serve with the mousse.

Serves 16

Curried Eggs

These make an appetizing first course, or serve them on a buffet table.

24 small eggs
1 pint (600 ml) good mayonnaise
4 tablespoons mango chutney sauce
2 tablespoons tomato chutney
salt
freshly ground black pepper
1 rounded teaspoon curry powder
dill and anchovy fillets to garnish

Hard-boil the eggs in boiling water for 10 minutes, cool under running cold water to prevent a line from forming around the yolk. Shell the eggs, halve them lengthwise and arrange them on a serving dish.

Mix all the remaining ingredients together until thoroughly blended, then spoon an even coating over the top of the eggs. Chill well before serving garnished with dill and anchovy fillets.

Serves 24 as a first course with salad

Celebration Salmon

Celebration Salmon

Use Scotch farmed salmon which is available all the year round at a reasonable price. For larger fish, between 7 and 10 lb (3.2-4.5 kg), bring to the boil, then simmer for 10-12 minutes in a fish kettle. If you don't possess a fish kettle, the fish can be baked in the oven. Remove the head, season well and wrap in buttered foil. Lift into a large meat tin, pour boiling water around the fish so that it comes halfway up the fish. Bake at 400°F/200°C/gas mark 6 for 10 minutes per pound (450 g), turning the fish in the foil halfway through the cooking. Leave in the foil to become luke-warm, then skin and bone the fish. It is best to use a light aspic, but you can use a can of consommé and ½ oz (12.5 g) of powdered gelatine.

To make a board for the salmon, simply measure the fish without the head and double the length and allow enough space for a parsley garnish. An old thick floorboard is ideal, cut to size and covered with foil.

5½ lb (2.5 kg) salmon, head removed and cleaned
2 heaped tablespoons salt
3 bay leaves
1 onion, sliced
12 peppercorns
4 tablespoons white wine vinegar
1 packet Swiss or Scandinavian aspic jelly powder, to make 1 pint (600 ml)
½ cucumber
8 oz (225 g) shelled prawns
fresh parsley or dill to garnish

Lift the salmon into a fish kettle, add salt, bay leaves, onion, peppercorns and vinegar. Add just enough water to cover the fish. Cover and bring slowly to the boil, then simmer for 5 minutes. Remove from the heat, leave until the fish is warm but not hot, about 4 hours.

Lift the fish out carefully onto a board, slide a knife just above the backbone along the length of the fish and lift the fillet onto a tray and peel off the skin. Remove the bones and skin from the second fillet. Cover.

both fillets with cling film and put in the freezer for about 1 hour until the fish is really cold.

While this is cooling, make up the aspic by following the instructions on the packet. I tend to use a little less water than the instructions say, then I make up the quantity with ice cubes to speed up the proceedings.

Slice the cucumber very thinly. Take the fish from the freezer, lift onto the serving board placing the widest ends of the fish in the centre, with the tails at each end to form a long diamond shape. Spoon over a thin layer of cold and thick, but not set, aspic. Arrange two parallel lines of cucumber the length of both fillets of salmon, leaving a space for the prawns. Add the prawns and a little chopped parsley to the remainder of the aspic and spoon down the centre of each fillet. Keep cold until ready to serve. Garnish with fresh parsley or dill.

Serves 10

Danish Honey Glazed Gammon

This is home cooked in the oven; no need to soak the joint unless you like it very mild. I tested an 8 lb (3.5 kg) piece of middle gammon and it was plenty for 20 people with a small portion of Mild Spiced Chicken Mayonnaise. I have also included cooking times for other sizes of bacon joints cooked in the oven.

8 lb (3.5 kg) joint of boneless
    middle gammon Danish bacon

For the glaze
4 tablespoons dark muscovado
    sugar
2 tablespoons runny honey
1 teaspoon made mustard

Rinse the joint, weigh and calculate cooking time:
joints up to 5 lb (2.3 kg) 35 minutes per pound (450 g) plus 35 minutes
5-7 lb (2.3-3 kg) 25 minutes per pound (450 g) plus 25 minutes
7-10 lb (3.2-4.5 kg) 20 minutes per pound (450 g) plus 40 minutes

Heat the oven to 350°F/180°C/gas mark 4. Wrap the joint in foil, put in a roasting tin, pour about an inch (2.5 cm) water in the bottom of the tin. Roast in the oven for the correct cooking time. Forty minutes before the end of cooking, remove the joint from the oven and cool for about 10 minutes. Carefully cut and pull off any strings and remove the rind with a sharp knife; the rind can be pulled back as it is cut. Mark the fat into a diamond pattern, mix the ingredients for the glaze together and spread over the gammon. Press the foil against the meat but leave the fat open, then return to the oven for the remaining cooking time until it is a pale golden brown all over the fat surface.

Serves 20

Danish Honey Glazed Gammon with Brown Rice Salad (see page 30)

Spinach, Cheese and Bacon Quiche

If possible, use the deepest flan tin you have as there is lots of filling. I prefer to buy the cheese that is already sliced for this.

For the pastry case
8 oz (225 g) plain flour
2 oz (50 g) lard
2 oz (50 g) margarine
about 2 good tablespoons water

For the filling
6 oz (175 g) streaky bacon, chopped
1 lb (454 g) packet frozen cut leaf
    spinach, thawed and drained
6 oz (175 g) Gruyère cheese, thinly
    sliced
4 eggs
¾ pint (450 ml) single cream
salt
freshly ground black pepper

Heat the oven to 425°F/220°C/gas mark 7 with a thick baking tray in it.

Put the flour in a bowl, add the fat cut into small pieces and rub in with the fingertips until the mixture resembles fine breadcrumbs. Bind together with sufficient water to form a firm dough. Roll out the pastry on a lightly floured surface and use to line a deep 11 inch (27.5 cm) flan tin. Chill for about 30 minutes. Line the flan with grease-proof paper and baking beans, bake blind for about 20 minutes, removing the paper and beans for the last 5 minutes so that the centre can cook through.

For the filling, gently cook the bacon in a pan over a low heat until the fat begins to run out, then increase the heat until the bacon is crisp. Spread spinach over the base of the flan case, arrange slices of cheese on top of the spinach. Scatter bacon over the cheese. Beat the eggs and blend with the cream and seasoning, then pour the egg mixture into the flan case. Reduce the oven to 350°F/180°C/gas mark 4 and cook the quiche for about 30 minutes until the filling has set. Serve either warm or cold.

Serves 10

Mushroom Mousse

This starter looks really attractive garnished with fresh watercress.

12 oz (350 g) button mushrooms
½ oz (12.5 g) powdered gelatine
4 tablespoons cold water
10 oz (275 g) can condensed
  consommé
2 oz (50 g) butter
½ pint (300 ml) whipping cream,
  whipped
½ pint (300 ml) good thick
  mayonnaise
½ teaspoon curry powder
salt
freshly ground black pepper

Put the gelatine in a small bowl with the water, leave to stand for about 3 minutes to form a sponge, then stand over a bowl of simmering water until the gelatine is clear. Remove from the heat and allow to cool. Add the gelatine to the consommé.

Melt the butter in a pan and fry the mushrooms for about 5 minutes until tender. Allow to cool before slicing finely. Stir the sliced mushrooms into the consommé. Pour about a quarter of the consommé into an oiled 2 pint (1.2 litre) ring mould. Chill in the refrigerator until set. When it has cooled sufficiently to be thick but not set, add to the remaining consommé the cream, mayonnaise, curry powder, salt and pepper. Mix until thoroughly blended and pour on top of the set consommé in the ring mould. Leave in the refrigerator until set. Just before serving, turn out and serve with toast and unsalted butter.

Serves 10

Spinach, Cheese and Bacon Quiche with Green Salad (see page 47)

Ham and Leek Quiche

This is a deliciously light quiche. Be sure to cook the pastry case right through before adding the filling.

For the pastry case
8 oz (225 g) pastry (see recipe for
  Spinach, Cheese and Bacon
  Quiche opposite)

For the filling
1½ oz (40 g) butter
3 leeks, finely sliced
10 thin slices ham
salt
freshly ground black pepper
4 eggs
½ pint (300 ml) single cream
½ pint (300 ml) milk

Prepare and cook the pastry case as in the recipe for Spinach, Cheese and Bacon Quiche. Reduce the oven to 350°F/180°C/gas mark 4.

For the filling, heat the butter in a pan and sauté the leeks for about 3 minutes until beginning to soften. Spoon these over the base of the pastry case. Roll the slices of ham into 'sausage' shapes and arrange like the spokes of a wheel in the flan case. Season well. Beat the eggs, blend in the cream and milk and pour into the flan case. Cook in the oven for about 35 minutes until the filling has set. Serve either warm or cold.

Serves 10

Whole Honey Glazed Ham

This recipe is really a bit of a cheat. When catering for a large number, I find it time-saving to use a boneless carving ham, which is in the shape of a traditional ham, but the joy being that it is boned and cooked. You can normally buy this from somewhere like Cash and Carry or order it from a delicatessen. However, if you do have difficulty in getting one, contact Mattessons, 173 Manor Road, West Ham, London E15 3DA. It is so simple to carve and looks wonderful with a home-made glaze.

9-10 lb (4-4.5 kg) boneless carving ham

For the glaze
4 oz (100 g) demerara sugar
1 tablespoon dry mustard
2 tablespoons runny honey

Remove the plastic wrap from the ham, then gently skim off the crumbed surface on the skin, taking off as little as possible. To make the home-made glaze, mix the sugar with the mustard and honey and spread over the ham. Wrap all the lean ham with foil and brown the joint in a very hot oven for about 10 minutes until golden brown all over. It may take a little longer, but do keep an eye on it.

A 10 lb (4.5 kg) ham will serve 25-30 people or more with other meats

Tomato and Onion Salad

This salad is always a favourite. For a very special occasion it is nice to take the skin off the tomatoes.

1½ lb (675 g) firm tomatoes
3 medium onions
6 tablespoons French dressing
chopped chives

Slice the tomatoes thinly. Very thinly slice the onions and arrange with the tomatoes in layers in a serving dish, finishing with a layer of tomatoes.

Spoon the French dressing over the salad and chill in the refrigerator until required. Just before serving, sprinkle with chopped chives.

Serves 10 with other salads

New Potato Salad

No need to peel the potatoes for this one.

2 lb (900 g) baby new potatoes
12 sprigs fresh mint
½ pint (300 ml) good thick mayonnaise
2 tablespoons freshly chopped chives
salt
freshly ground black pepper

Scrub the potatoes clean, then cook in boiling salted water with the mint for about 15 minutes or until just tender. Drain and allow to cool. Put the potatoes in a bowl and mix with mayonnaise, chives and plenty of seasoning until evenly coated. Turn into a serving dish and chill well before serving.

Serve 10 with other salads

Cucumber and Dill Salad

This is a refreshing salad which goes particularly well with fish.

2 cucumbers
2 tablespoons sunflower oil
4 tablespoons hot water
4 tablespoons white wine vinegar
4 tablespoons caster sugar
1 teaspoon salt
freshly ground black pepper
chopped fresh dill

Peel the cucumbers, cut into thin slices and arrange in a serving dish.

Blend the oil, water, vinegar, sugar and seasoning together and pour over the cucumber. Sprinkle with dill and serve.

Serves 10 with other salads

Danish Potato Salad

Decorate with fresh dill if you have some.

2 lb (900 g) old potatoes, peeled
12 tablespoons French dressing
½ pint (300 ml) good thick mayonnaise
4 dill pickles, chopped
2 red dessert apples, cored and chopped
juice of 1 lemon
salt
freshly ground black pepper

Cook the potatoes in boiling salted water for about 20 minutes until just tender. Drain and allow to cool until just cool enough to handle, dice and toss in French dressing while still warm. Chill in the refrigerator for about 2 hours, then stir in the mayonnaise and dill pickles. Mix the chopped apple with the lemon juice to prevent it from discolouring and stir into the potato mixture with plenty of seasoning. Transfer to a serving dish and chill well before serving.

Serves 10 with other salads

Brown Rice Salad

This salad is delicious without being dressed, but if liked stir in a little French dressing. If you are not too fond of the texture of brown rice, use half the quantity of brown rice and half long-grain rice. Cook separately, as they have different cooking times, then mix them together.

1 lb (450 g) brown rice
15 oz (425 g) can chick peas,
   drained
8 oz (225 g) sultanas
4 oz (100 g) walnut pieces
2 large sticks celery, chopped
salt
freshly ground black pepper

Cook the rice in boiling salted water as directed by the manufacturer on the packet. Brown rice does take longer to cook than ordinary long-grain rice. Rinse well under running cold water, drain well and allow to cool. Stir in the chick peas, sultanas, walnuts, celery and plenty of seasoning. Turn into a large bowl for serving. Serve well chilled.

Serves 20 with other salads

Good Thick Mayonnaise

This is so quick and easy to make as it is all done in a processor or blender.

2 eggs
1 tablespoon white wine vinegar
1 teaspoon caster sugar
1 teaspoon dry mustard
1 teaspoon salt
freshly ground black pepper
about 1 pint (600 ml) sunflower oil
juice of 1 large lemon

Put all the ingredients, except the oil and lemon juice in a processor or blender. Switch to a low speed to blend. Increase the speed to maximum and add the oil in a slow steady stream until the mixture is very thick and all the oil has been absorbed. Add the lemon juice and process again until thoroughly mixed.

Taste and check seasoning, then turn into a bowl to serve.

Herb Mayonnaise

To ½ pint (300 ml) mayonnaise add 2 tablespoons double cream and 2 tablespoons freshly chopped herbs.

Green Pasta Salad

This simple combination is good with other salads for a buffet.

8 oz (225 g) green tagliatelle
15 oz (425 g) can red kidney beans,
   drained
8 oz (225 g) shelled prawns
¼ pint (150 ml) good thick
   mayonnaise
1 teaspoon paprika pepper
salt
freshly ground black pepper

Cook the pasta in boiling salted water for about 10 minutes until just tender. Rinse thoroughly with hot water, drain well and allow to cool. Stir in the kidney beans, prawns, mayonnaise, paprika, salt and black pepper. Toss well until evenly coated, then turn into a large serving bowl and chill well.

Serves 20 with other salads

Green Pasta Salad

French Dressing

1 clove garlic, crushed
1 teaspoon dry mustard
1 teaspoon salt
freshly ground black pepper
2 teaspoons caster sugar
½ pint (300 ml) sunflower oil
¼ pint (150 ml) white wine vinegar

Blend the first five ingredients together in a bowl, then gradually mix in the oil with a whisk. Stir in the vinegar, taste and adjust seasoning if necessary.

ANNIVERSARY DINNER PARTIES

It is fun to have a colour scheme for a menu. The following menu
has a golden theme so is ideal for a golden wedding, but would do equally well for
any special meal.

Prawns in mayonnaise wrapped in smoked salmon
or Orange and carrot soup
Beef Wellington with mushroom Madeira sauce
or Creamed chicken curry with mango
Apricot and orange mousse, An excellent trifle
or Canadian peach pie

A natural first course for a ruby wedding is smoked salmon pâté.
The main course could be a cold buffet, including rare cold beef
with lettuce and radichio salad (radichio is a heavenly ruby colour).
Or perhaps game pie (see page 43) with red cabbage. The
puddings, if you want ruby red ones, are almost bound to be fruity.

Prawns in Mayonnaise wrapped in Smoked Salmon

Thaw the prawns slowly in the refrigerator overnight, drain really well on kitchen paper.

1 lb (450 g) frozen peeled prawns, thawed
½ pint (300 ml) good thick mayonnaise
salt
freshly ground black pepper
1 lb (450 g) smoked salmon, sliced
crisp lettuce leaves
fresh dill
10 lemon wedges

Put the prawns in a bowl, add the mayonnaise, season well and toss until evenly coated. Cut the smoked salmon slices in half, divide the prawns between them and roll up to form sausage shapes. Cut each sausage shape into about 2 inch (5 cm) lengths. Take 10 small plates, arrange lettuce leaves and 3 salmon rolls on each plate. Decorate with dill and a wedge of lemon and serve with granary bread and unsalted butter.

Serves 10

Smoked Salmon Pâté

Either make one large pâté or divide the mixture into individual serving dishes for a more personal effect.

1 lb (450 g) smoked salmon pieces
8 oz (225 g) rich cream cheese
8 oz (225 g) butter, melted
freshly ground black pepper
a little salt
juice of ½ lemon
parsley and tomato wedges to garnish

Topping
1 oz (25 g) butter

Put the salmon pieces, cream cheese, butter, seasoning and lemon juice in a blender or processor and reduce to a purée. If your machine is small, do this in batches. Check seasoning.

Turn into a 2 pint (1.2 litre) dish and level the top. Melt the butter for the topping, pour over the top and chill well until set. Take out of the refrigerator about an hour before serving, garnish with parsley and tomato wedges. Serve with brown bread toast and unsalted butter.

Serves 10 as a first course

Carrot and Orange Soup

2 lb (1 kg) carrots, peeled and sliced
2 lb (1 kg) onions, sliced
2 oz (50 g) butter
2½ pints (1.5 litres) chicken stock
½ pint (300 ml) orange juice
1 bay leaf
salt
freshly ground black pepper
chopped parsley to garnish

Gently fry the carrots and onions in the butter in a pan for about 10 minutes until the onions are tender. Pour on the stock and the orange juice, add the bay leaf and seasoning. Bring to the boil, cover with a lid and simmer for about 20 minutes until the carrots are tender. Remove the bay leaf, then purée in a processor or blender until smooth. Taste and check seasoning. Pour the soup back into a pan and reheat until piping hot before serving in a large tureen garnished with chopped parsley.

Serves 10

Mushroom Madeira Sauce

Make the sauce ahead of time, then reheat and stir in the cream.

2 oz (50 g) butter
1 small onion, finely chopped
8 oz (225 g) mushrooms, finely chopped
1½ oz (40 g) flour
¾ pint (450 ml) good beef stock, including the juices from the meat
3 tablespoons Madeira
salt
freshly ground black pepper
¼ pint (150 ml) single cream

Heat the butter in a pan and gently fry the onion for about 5 minutes until beginning to soften, add the mushrooms and cook for a further 2 minutes. Add the flour and cook for a minute, then gradually blend in the stock and the reserved meat juices, stirring until thickened. Reduce the sauce to a purée in a processor or blender and stir in the Madeira. Rinse out the pan, return the sauce to the pan and season to taste. Reheat until boiling, remove from the heat and stir in the cream. Taste and check seasoning. Serve immediately with the fillet of beef (see page 34).

Serves 10

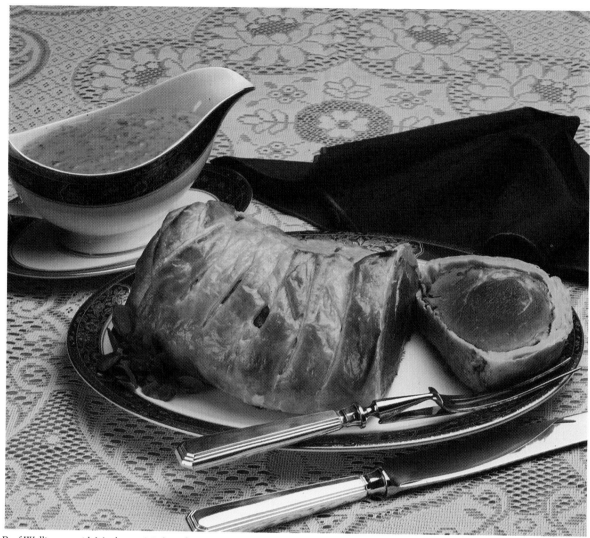

Beef Wellington with Mushroom Madeira Sauce (see page 33)

Beef Wellington

Get the butcher to cut the fillet from the thick end and ask him to string it at intervals to give a good shape.

3½ lb (1.5 kg) trimmed fillet of beef
2 oz (50 g) butter
1 tablespoon sunflower oil
salt
freshly ground black pepper
14 oz (400 g) packet frozen puff
    pastry, thawed
a little beaten egg to glaze

Heat the oven to 425°F/220°C/gas mark 7. Heat the butter and oil in a roasting tin for a few minutes before adding the fillet. Season well with salt and pepper and roast in the oven for 20-30 minutes (20 minutes for rare and 30 minutes for medium-done meat), turning the meat round in the fat every 7-8 minutes. Lift the meat out of the tin and leave to go cold. Save the juices for the sauce.

Remove the string from around the joint. Roll out the pastry on a lightly floured surface to a rectangle three times as wide as the beef and about 4 inches (10 cm) longer. Lay the fillet in the middle of the pastry, cut strips about ½ inch (1.25 cm) wide of pastry diagonally to the meat on each side and brush with egg. Plait strips across the meat by alternately lifting strips from each side over the meat. Or just simply wrap the meat in pastry, seal and decorate with leaves from the pastry trimmings. Chill in the refrigerator until ready to cook.

Bake in the oven at 425°F/220°C/gas mark 7 for about 30 minutes until the pastry is well risen and a golden brown. Lift onto a serving plate and serve at once with Mushroom Madeira Sauce (see page 33).

Serves 10

Creamed Chicken Curry with Mango

Serve this very mild creamy spiced chicken with boiled rice: 1¼ lb (550 g) raw rice is enough for 10 people. Add fried almonds and fried chopped red and green pepper to the rice just before serving.

To make ahead, complete up to the sauce stage. Blend a quarter of the sauce with the chicken, cover and chill. Put the rest of the sauce in another container in the fridge. Half an hour before serving, gently reheat the chicken in the sauce in a nonstick pan. Beat the remaining sauce until smooth, add to the chicken and continue reheating. Keep hot in a low oven. Add the mango at the last moment.

6 lb (2.7 kg) chicken
1 large onion
2 bay leaves
a bunch of parsley stalks
1 level teaspoon salt
plenty of freshly ground black pepper
2 pints (1.2 litres) sweet cider
2½ oz (62.5 g) butter
1 level tablespoon curry powder
1 teaspoon ground turmeric
1½ oz (40 g) flour
1 chicken stock cube
1 tablespoon redcurrant jelly
½ pint (300 ml) single cream
2 large ripe mangoes

Put the chicken in a large pan with the onion, bay leaves, parsley, salt and pepper. Pour over the cider, cover the pan with a lid and simmer gently for about 1¼ hours until the chicken is tender.

Lift the chicken from the pan and leave until just cool enough to handle. Boil the stock rapidly until reduced to 1 pint (600 ml), strain, skim off the surplus fat and put to one side. Remove the flesh from the chicken, cut into neat pieces, place in a serving dish and keep warm.

Melt the butter in a pan, stir in the curry powder and turmeric and cook gently for 2 minutes. Stir in the flour and cook for a minute. Slowly blend in the stock, add the stock cube and bring to the boil, stirring. Add the redcurrant jelly and simmer for 2-3 minutes, check seasoning. Remove the sauce from the heat and stir in the cream.

Peel the mangoes and cut slices of mango in wedge shapes going round the stone. Stir the least perfect wedges into the sauce just before serving and decorate with 10 slices of mango so each person gets one.

Serves 10

Prawns in Mayonnaise wrapped in Smoked Salmon (see page 33) and Creamed Chicken Curry with Mango

Ruby Fruit Salad

Just before serving, stir in a little brandy to taste and serve with cream – delicious!

8 oz (225 g) rhubarb, cut in ¾ inch (2 cm) lengths
8 oz (225 g) blackcurrants
8 oz (225 g) granulated sugar
6 tablespoons water
8 oz (225 g) small strawberries, hulled
8 oz (225 g) raspberries

Put the rhubarb in a saucepan with the blackcurrants. Add the sugar and water and bring to the boil, then simmer until barely tender, stirring continuously – this will take only a few minutes. Add the strawberries and raspberries and cook for a further minute. Turn into a serving dish and chill well before serving with lashings of cream.

Apricot and Orange Chantilly

The colour of this delicious mousse is just perfect for a golden wedding celebration.

8 oz (225 g) dried apricot pieces
1 pint (600 ml) water
½ oz (12.5 g) gelatine
4 tablespoons cold water
4 oz (100 g) caster sugar
4 eggs
6 fl oz (175 ml) frozen orange juice, thawed
¾ pint (450 ml) whipping cream, whipped

Put the apricots in a bowl with the water and allow to stand overnight. Transfer the apricots and water to a pan and simmer gently for about 10 minutes until tender. Purée through a sieve or process in a blender or food processor. Allow to cool.

Put the gelatine in a bowl with the cold water and allow to stand for about 3 minutes to form a sponge. Put the bowl in a pan of simmering water and allow the gelatine to dissolve. Whisk the eggs and the caster sugar with an electric whisk on full speed until the whisk leaves a trail when it is lifted out of the mixture. Stir in the cooled gelatine, orange juice, apricot purée and ½ pint (300 ml) whipped cream, stir and gently fold until blended. Pour into a large glass serving bowl and leave in the refrigerator to set. Decorate with the rest of the whipped cream.

Serves 10

Ruby Fruit Salad and Loganberry Mousse

Canadian Peach Pie

This is a truly fabulous pie given to me by a very special Canadian girlfriend. To skin the peaches, plunge into boiling water for a few moments until the skin peels off easily – it is easiest to hold the peach on the end of a fork.

For the pastry case
8 oz (225 g) plain flour
3 oz (75 g) lard
3 oz (75 g) butter
1 oz (25 g) caster sugar
1 egg yolk
about 2 tablespoons water

For the filling
4 oz (100 g) caster sugar
2 oz (50 g) light muscovado sugar
8 fresh peaches, skinned, stoned and sliced
3 level tablespoons cornflour
1/4 teaspoon ground nutmeg
1/4 teaspoon ground cinnamon
1 oz (25 g) butter
juice of 1/2 lemon
a little beaten egg to glaze

Heat the oven to 425°F/220°C/gas mark 7. Put a thick metal baking sheet on the middle shelf to heat up with the oven; this ensures the underneath of the pastry will be really crisp when the pie is baked.

Prepare the pastry. Put the flour in a bowl and rub in the lard and butter until the mixture resembles fine breadcrumbs, stir in the sugar, egg yolk and water and bind together to form a firm dough. Use two-thirds of the pastry to line a 9 inch (22.5 cm) loose-bottomed, fluted flan tin.

To make the filling, combine the two sugars together in a bowl, add the peach slices and mix well until evenly coated with sugar. Leave to stand for at least an hour, then strain off and reserve the liquid. Measure the cornflour into a small pan, mix in the nutmeg and cinnamon and blend in the reserved liquid from the peaches. Cook over a gentle heat until thick, stirring continuously. Remove from the heat and stir in the butter and lemon juice. Combine the peaches with this sauce and arrange in the pastry case. Roll out the remaining pastry, cut into strips and use to make a lattice pattern on top of the pie. Glaze with a little beaten egg. Bake in the oven for 20 minutes, then reduce the oven to 350°F/180°C/gas mark 4 for a further 20 minutes until the pastry is cooked through. Serve warm with thick cream.

Serves 10

An Excellent Trifle

This is a boozy one, but now the children are older we all love it for special family occasions. The custard is a good way of using up the yolks when you have made meringues for the same do.

2 packets trifle sponges
strawberry jam
2 crushed macaroons
2 × 15 oz (425 g) cans pear halves, drained and juice reserved
8 tablespoons inexpensive sherry

For the custard
6 egg yolks
2 oz (50 g) caster sugar
2 heaped teaspoons cornflour
1 pint (600 ml) milk

Topping
1/2 pint (300 ml) whipping cream, whipped
browned flaked almonds

Split the sponges, spread with strawberry jam and sandwich them together. Cut each sponge into 6 small squares and use to line the bottom of a shallow 12 inch (30 cm) glass bowl, scatter over the macaroons. Arrange the pears on top of the sponges and press down to give an even surface. Mix the sherry with reserved pear juice and pour over the sponges.

For the custard, mix together the egg yolks, sugar and cornflour. Heat the milk in a pan until hand hot, then pour onto the egg yolks, stirring continuously. Return the mixture to the pan and cook gently, stirring until thickened. Cool, whisk in a processor or blender or with an electric whisk for a few moments until light. Pour on top of the trifle and allow to set completely. Top with the whipped cream, decorate with almonds and chill really well before serving.

Serves 10

Loganberry Mousse

The colour of this mousse is just perfect for a ruby wedding celebration, but be sure to use it on other occasions too!

2 × 15 oz (425 g) cans loganberries
2 packets raspberry jelly
15 oz (425 g) can evaporated milk, really well chilled
juice of 1/2 lemon
whipped cream to decorate

Strain the juice from the loganberries and make up to 1 pint (600 ml) with water. Put the juice in a pan and bring up to boiling point. Add the jelly in small pieces and stir until dissolved. Leave in a cold place until just beginning to set.

Sieve the loganberries. Put the evaporated milk and lemon juice in a bowl and whisk until it begins to form soft peaks. Fold the loganberry purée and evaporated milk into the half set jelly. Mix well until thoroughly blended, then pour into a serving dish. Chill well before serving. Decorate with whipped cream.

Serves 10

ANNIVERSARY DINNER FOR SIX

For this small party I suggest that half a duck is served for
each person. Duck is so delicious but there is not an abundance
of meat on the bird. This makes for easy carving too; the birds are
just split down the middle and the bulky backbone snipped
off with kitchen scissors. As the duck is rich, the first course is
light and simple. For pudding, choose religieuses (see page 56) or
paniers russes, crisp biscuit baskets, filled with ginger ice cream.
Lay the table as far in advance as you can (I like to do this a day
ahead and shut off the dining area – the family then have to
eat in the kitchen!). Choose a colour scheme to suit the occasion
and match the candles, flowers and napkins. A brightly-coloured,
dyed old cotton sheet looks fabulous under a lace
bedspread or cloth (don't forget mats underneath so
your table is not marked by hot dishes).

Two Melons and Tomato in Mint Dressing

It is essential to serve this really cold. To skin tomatoes, plunge in very hot water for a few moments before peeling; the skin will then slip off easily.

1 small honeydew melon
1 small cantaloupe melon
8 oz (225 g) tomatoes

For the dressing
6 sprigs fresh mint
3 teaspoons caster sugar
1 tablespoon white wine vinegar
1 tablespoon lemon juice
6 tablespoons sunflower oil
salt
freshly ground black pepper

Cut both melons in half and remove the seeds. Scoop out the flesh with a melon baller. Skin and quarter the tomatoes and remove the seeds and discard. Mix the tomato with the melon.

For the dressing, chop the mint very finely and mix with the sugar, vinegar, lemon juice, oil, salt and pepper. Pour over the melon and tomatoes, cover and leave in the refrigerator for about 5 hours until really cold. Taste and check seasoning. Serve in individual glasses or half a melon shell, garnished with mint and accompanied by hot garlic rolls or bread.

Serves 6

Two Melons and Tomato in Mint Dressing

Roast Duck with Cherry Sauce (see page 40)

Roast Duck with Cherry Sauce

Duck is so delicious but there is not much meat, so for this special occasion serve half a duck for each person.

3 ducks, about 3½ lb (1.5 kg) each
watercress to garnish

For the sauce
2 level teaspoons arrowroot
14 oz (397 g) can stoned black cherries, with juice reserved
4 tablespoons inexpensive port
juice of ½ orange
salt
freshly ground black pepper

Heat the oven to 375°F/190°C/gas mark 5. Remove the giblets from the birds, rub a little salt into the skin and stand the ducks, breast side up, on a wire rack in a roasting tin. Open roast in the oven, allowing 30 minutes per pound (450 g) for each duck, until the ducks are tender and the skin is golden brown and crisp. If necessary, turn the oven temperature up at the very end of cooking to get the skin crisp.

For the sauce, measure the arrowroot into a pan, gradually blend in the juice from the cherries, bring to the boil, stirring until thickened. Stir in the cherries, port, orange juice, seasoning and the skimmed juices (with fat removed) from the roasting tin. Taste and check the seasoning, then serve with the roast ducks.

To serve the ducks, take a sharp pair of kitchen scissors. Turn one duck over on its breast, snip down either side of the backbone, lift away from the bird and discard. Snip through the breast to divide the bird into two, repeat with the other ducks. Arrange on a large heated platter, garnished with a little sauce and watercress. Serve the rest of the sauce separately.

Serves 6

Very Special Ginger Ice Cream

If you have stem ginger left from Christmas, this is a perfect way of serving it and this is ideal too for a golden wedding celebration.

4 eggs, separated
1 level teaspoon ground ginger
4 oz (100 g) stem ginger, chopped
4 oz (100 g) caster sugar
½ pint (300 ml) whipping cream

Whisk the egg yolks and ginger in a small bowl until blended. In a larger bowl whisk the egg whites with an electric whisk until stiff, then whisk in the sugar a teaspoonful at a time. The whites will get stiffer and stiffer as the sugar is added. Blend in the yolks and ginger until there are no streaks of colour. Whisk the cream until it forms peaks and fold into the ginger mixture. Turn into a 2½ pint (1.4 litre) container. Cover and freeze until solid. To serve, leave at room temperature for about 5 minutes before serving in small scoops in the paniers russes.

Fills 8-10 cups

Paniers Russes

These biscuit cups are perfect for serving ice creams and sorbets in; three small scoops look beautiful decorated with fresh fruits. They can also be used for serving fresh fruits and whipped cream.

2 oz (50 g) butter
2½ oz (62.5 g) caster sugar
2 egg whites
2 oz (50 g) plain flour

Heat the oven to 425°F/220°C/gas mark 7. Grease two baking sheets very well with white cooking fat or lard.

Cream the butter and sugar together until light, then gradually beat in the egg whites until all added. Fold in the flour, spoon the mixture in heaped teaspoonfuls onto the greased baking trays and spread out with the back of the spoon to about 3 inch (7.5 cm) circles. Allow two circles of mixture per tray. Bake trays one at a time in the oven for 3-4 minutes or until the biscuits are just tinged with brown around the edge. As soon as the biscuits come out of the oven, lift them off the trays with a palette knife and press into a breakfast cup or small bowl. These biscuits begin to crisp very quickly as they cool, so don't bake too many at a time otherwise they become difficult to handle. Repeat with the remaining mixture.

Makes about 15 cups

HOT, SAVOURY BUFFET FOOD

All these dishes may be eaten with a fork. Serve the moussaka
or lasagne with a green salad and French bread. The game pie goes
well with red cabbage or mixed broccoli and cauliflower
florets and creamy mashed potato. You might like to have some
buttered carrots and celeriac as well, as not everyone likes the
same vegetables. Don't serve both moussaka and lasagne for the
same party as they are too alike. I find it best to give a choice of
only two hot dishes; more take too long to serve, as friends take
ages to make up their minds! Make sure the food is piping hot
and the plates are not too hot to handle. If you are short of
hotplates or oven space to heat them, a dishwasher might help —
some dishwashers have a plate-warming cycle, or give plates
a short hot wash just before they are needed. When the course
is over, collect all the plates and stack them neatly in the
kitchen before progressing. It's amazing how many guests
appear in the kitchen, so keep clutter to the minimum!
First courses should be simple — perhaps a bowl of soup or something
in an individual dish, such as an avocado or smoked fish mousse,
or perhaps some beautiful, small, smoked salmon open sandwiches.

Lasagne

This is ideal cooked in foil dishes, particularly if freezing the dish, as it can be reheated straight from the freezer once thawed. A thin pre-cooked lasagne, such as Barilla's, is best for this recipe. If thick pasta is used, it will not cook in time.

about 8 oz (225 g) precooked
  lasagne
1 oz (25 g) Parmesan cheese

Meat sauce
1 lb (450 g) raw minced beef
1 lb (450 g) raw minced pork
4 oz (100 g) bacon pieces, chopped
12 oz (350 g) onions, chopped
about 8 large sticks celery, chopped
1½ oz (40 g) flour
¾ pint (450 ml) stock
8 oz (225 g) tomato purée
2 fat cloves garlic, crushed
1 tablespoon redcurrant jelly
salt
freshly ground black pepper

White sauce
3 oz (75 g) butter
3 oz (75 g) flour
freshly grated nutmeg
salt
freshly ground black pepper
1½ pints (900 ml) milk
1 teaspoon made mustard
6 oz (175 g) Gruyère cheese
2 oz (50 g) well-flavoured Cheddar
  cheese

To make the meat sauce, put the beef, pork and bacon in a pan. Heat gently until the fat runs, then increase the heat and fry until browned. Add the chopped onions and celery and cook for 5 minutes. Stir in the flour, add the remaining ingredients and bring to the boil. Reduce the heat, cover with a lid and simmer for about an hour until the meat is cooked.

For the white sauce, melt the butter in a pan and stir in the flour, nutmeg, salt and pepper and cook for 2 minutes, stirring. Add the milk gradually and stir over the heat until thickened. Add the mustard and check seasoning. Combine the Gruyère and Cheddar cheeses.

In a shallow 4 pint (2.3 litre) casserole or meat tin put a third of the meat sauce, the white sauce and the cheese, followed by half the lasagne. Try not to overlap the lasagne. Start again with layers of meat, white sauce and cheese, ending with cheese on top. Sprinkle a little grated Parmesan on top.

Heat the oven to 350°F/180°C/gas mark 4. Cook in the oven for about 50 minutes to an hour or until the top is brown and bubbling.

Serves 10

Chicken in Soured Cream with Chives

If you use a pyrex or china casserole, transfer the sauce to a pan to thicken.

10 chicken breasts, skinned and
  boned
1 oz (25 g) butter
2 tablespoons sunflower oil
2 large onions, chopped
6 fl oz (175 ml) frozen concentrated
  orange juice, thawed
½ pint (300 ml) chicken stock
2 tablespoons chopped fresh chives
salt
freshly ground black pepper
½ oz (12.5 g) cornflour
2 tablespoons water
½ pint (300 ml) soured cream
wedges of orange and watercress
  to garnish

Heat the oven to 350°F/180°C/gas mark 4.

Heat the butter and oil in a pan and brown the chicken breasts on all sides, lift out of the pan and put into a 3 pint (1.7 litre) ovenproof casserole. Add the onions to the juices remaining in the pan and cook gently for about 3 minutes until beginning to soften, then stir in the orange juice, stock and chives. Season well. Bring to the boil and pour over the chicken. Cover the casserole with a lid and cook in the oven for about 30 minutes until the chicken is tender. Baste occasionally during cooking with the orange sauce.

Lift the chicken out of the casserole and arrange on a warmed serving dish. Blend the cornflour with the water in a small bowl, stir into the orange sauce and bring back to the boil, stirring until thickened. Allow to cool slightly before stirring in the soured cream. Pour over the chicken and serve garnished with wedges of orange and watercress.

Serves 10

Basic Marinade for Game

½ pint (300 ml) red wine
2 bay leaves
8 peppercorns
2 cloves garlic, halved
2 tablespoons sunflower oil
1 onion, sliced

Put all the ingredients in a large glass bowl. Add the meat, mix well, cover with cling film and store in the refrigerator for 1-2 days, turning the meat frequently. When ready to use, lift out the meat, discard any peppercorns or garlic sticking to the meat, strain the marinade and use in the sauce to serve with the meat.

Game Pie

This can be made in advance and frozen with the raw pastry, then thawed and baked when needed.

1 lb (450 g) venison, cubed
3 pigeons
1 lb (450 g) casserole pheasant
½ pint (300 ml) marinade (see basic marinade for game)
6 oz (175 g) fatty bacon, cubed
4 oz (100 g) German smoked sausage, skinned and sliced
1 large onion, chopped
2 oz (50 g) flour
about 1 pint (600 ml) beef stock
1 sprig fresh thyme
1½ tablespoons bramble jelly
salt
freshly ground black pepper
a dash of gravy browning

Pastry topping
14 oz (400 g) packet frozen puff pastry, thawed
beaten egg to glaze

Put the venison, pigeons and pheasant in a large glass or china bowl and pour over the marinade, cover with cling film and leave to marinate for 24 hours in the refrigerator. Lift the meat out of the marinade, strain and reserve the liquid. Discard the pieces of garlic, peppercorns, onion and bay leaf.

Put the bacon in a nonstick pan, cook slowly to draw out the fat. Add the sliced sausage and onion and cook for about 10 minutes until the bacon is crispy, add the flour and mix well.

Make the reserved wine marinade up to 1½ pints (900 ml) with stock, stir into the pan and bring to the boil, stirring until thickened. Add the venison, pigeons, pheasant, thyme and bramble jelly. Season well, add gravy browning, cover and simmer gently for about 2½ hours until tender; this could be longer if any of the birds are tough, so take out those that are done and continue to cook the remainder until tender. Cut the meat

from the pheasant and pigeons, discard the bones and thyme and return the meat to the sauce. Check seasoning. Put a pie funnel in the centre of a 3½ pint (2 litre) pie dish, add the meat and leave to become quite cold.

Roll out the pastry on a floured surface, use to cover the pie. Roll out trimmings and use to make leaves to decorate the pie. Glaze with a little beaten egg and bake in the oven at 425°F/220°C/gas mark 7 for about 20 minutes and then reduce the oven to 350°F/180°C/gas mark 4 for a further 30 minutes until the meat is piping hot and the pastry a golden brown. Serve with red cabbage or mixed florets of broccoli and cauliflower.

Serves 10

Florentine Pancakes

These spinach pancakes can form part of a hot buffet or be served on their own with French bread and unsalted butter.

Batter
8 oz (225 g) flour
2 eggs
1 pint (600 ml) milk
2 tablespoons sunflower oil
oil for frying

For the sauce
3 oz (75 g) butter
3 oz (75 g) flour
2 pints (1.2 litres) milk
salt
freshly ground black pepper
1 teaspoon Dijon mustard
a little ground nutmeg
8 oz (225 g) Cheddar cheese, grated

For the filling
3 lb (1.5 kg) frozen chopped leaf spinach, thawed and drained
6 oz (175 g) fresh white breadcrumbs
6 eggs, beaten
salt
freshly ground black pepper
4 oz (100 g) ham, diced

Start by preparing the pancakes. Put the flour in a bowl, make a well in the centre. Add the eggs and gradually stir in half the milk. Using a whisk, blend in the flour from the sides of the bowl, beat well until the mixture is smooth and stir in the remaining milk and sunflower oil. Heat a little oil in an 8 inch (20 cm) pan. When it is hot, pour off excess oil and spoon about 2 tablespoons of batter into the pan. Tip and rotate the pan so that the batter spreads out evenly and thinly covers the base. Cook for about a minute until pale brown underneath, turn over with a palette knife and cook for another minute. Slip the pancake out of the pan and make 19 more pancakes with the remaining batter.

For the sauce, heat the butter in a pan, stir in the flour and cook for a minute. Gradually blend in the milk and bring to the boil, stirring until thickened. Season well with salt and pepper. Pour ½ pint (300 ml) of the sauce into a bowl ready for the filling. Add the mustard, nutmeg and cheese to the remainder of the sauce. Leave on one side.

For the filling, add the spinach, breadcrumbs, eggs, salt, pepper and ham to the sauce in the bowl. Mix well until thoroughly blended. Spread the pancakes flat, spoon some of the filling on to each and roll them up like a sausage. Arrange the pancakes on a large flat ovenproof serving dish, and pour the cheese sauce over the top.

Heat the oven to 375°F/190°C/gas mark 5, bake the pancakes for about 30 minutes until heated through and the sauce is bubbling.

Serves 10

Moussaka

I no longer fry the aubergines first as I find it makes the dish far too fatty. I blanch them in water instead – but it is essential to drain the slices well afterwards.

2 lb (900 g) minced lamb
1 lb (450 g) onions, chopped
4 cloves garlic, crushed
3 oz (75 g) flour
salt
freshly ground black pepper
a little fresh or dried thyme
2 × 14 oz (397 g) cans tomatoes
8 small aubergines
chopped parsley to garnish

For the sauce
3 oz (75 g) butter
3 oz (75 g) flour
1½ pints (900 ml) milk
2 level teaspoons English made
    mustard
grated nutmeg
salt
freshly ground black pepper
10 oz (275 g) Cheddar cheese,
    grated
2 eggs, beaten

Heat the oven to 375°F/190°C/gas mark 5. Butter a very large or two smaller ovenproof dishes.

Turn the minced lamb into a large pan, cook over a low heat at first to let the fat run out of the meat and stir to avoid sticking. When the fat has freely run from the meat, add the onions and garlic and increase the heat. Fry to brown the meat for about 15 minutes. If there seems to be a surplus of fat, spoon it off. Add the flour, stir well, then add salt, pepper, thyme and the contents from the cans of tomatoes. Bring to the boil and simmer for about 5 minutes. Check seasoning.

Slice the aubergines and blanch in a pan of boiling water for 1 minute – this softens the skin and prevents the aubergines discolouring. Drain them dry on kitchen paper.

Make the sauce by slowly melting the butter in a pan, add the flour and cook for a minute. Blend in the milk, and bring to the boil, stirring well. Add the mustard, nutmeg, salt, pepper and cheese. Allow the cheese to melt, remove from the heat, add the eggs and mix well.

Now assemble the moussaka. First put a layer of half of the meat mixture in the dish, cover with half the aubergines and season. Repeat with the rest of the lamb and aubergines and pour over the cheese sauce. Bake uncovered in the oven for about 45-60 minutes until golden brown. Sprinkle with chopped parsley and serve hot.

Serves 10

A Good Party Punch

Must be served really well chilled. Chill unopened bottles overnight.

7 pints (4 litres) inexpensive white
    German wine, chilled
5½ pints (3 litres) lemonade,
    chilled
1¾ pints (1 litre) medium sweet
    cider, chilled
3 fl oz (85 ml) brandy
1 pint (600 ml) tray ice cubes
8 oz (225 g) small whole
    strawberries, hulled
a few sprigs of mint
2 green apples, cored and sliced

Mix all the ingredients together in a large punch bowl. Serve really cold.

Serves about 80 glasses

Cambridge Spiced Pork

This is a rich spicy casserole made from casserole pork which is now often available midweek in supermarkets – it is best to order it to be sure. This is just right for a crowd, served with boiled rice or creamy mashed potato and a green salad. It also freezes very well.

4 lb (1.8 kg) casserole pork, cubed
2 tablespoons sunflower oil
1 lb (450 g) onions, roughly
    chopped
3 cloves garlic, crushed
2½ oz (62.5 g) flour
2 level teaspoons curry powder
1 teaspoon ground ginger
2 × 1¾ lb (800 g) cans
    tomatoes
1 pint (600 ml) dry cider
salt
freshly ground black pepper

Heat the oven to 325°F/160°C/gas mark 3.

Measure the oil into a large nonstick frying pan. Fry the meat in two batches, browning on all sides, lift out with a slotted spoon and transfer the meat to an ovenproof casserole. Add the onions and garlic to the juices remaining in the pan and cook until lightly browned. Sprinkle in the flour, curry powder and ginger, cook for a minute, then blend in the tomatoes and cider and bring to the boil, stirring until thickened. Season well and pour over the pork. Cook in the oven covered with a lid for about 2 hours until the meat is tender.

Serves 10-12

Cambridge Spiced Pork

OPEN AIR FOOD

Food eaten out of doors always tastes better. Many of the ideas from the cold buffet could be used for a picnic as well as the ideas that follow. If you are going no distance, a beautiful plate of hors d'oeuvre, carefully wrapped in cling film, looks spectacular. It is essential that cold food is served cold: chill all drinks ahead, then pack in cool boxes or vacuum flasks. Salads too need to be cool to be crisp. If a tossed salad is being taken on a picnic, pack all the salad in one container and the dressing in another and toss just before handing round. Remember the extras like the bunch of watercress for decoration or the grapes to go with the cheeseboard. Put in a few savoury things like salted almonds for everyone to enjoy with a drink while the feast is being unpacked. Don't forget a bag for the rubbish and lots of paper napkins and kitchen roll too. If the weather is unsettled, take soup and hot coffee and perhaps a lovely fruit cake. I enjoy the simnel cake at any time of year. It is difficult to give quantities for a picnic as there are so many types of food to choose from. For each person, allow either a slice of quiche or pie or 4 oz (100 g) of cold meat, portions of two different salads plus a bread roll or piece of French bread, and a piece of cake or fresh fruit.

Wonderful Green Soup

Sorrel has a very strong characteristic flavour so you don't have to use very much. Serve either piping hot or well chilled.

1 lb (450 g) fresh spinach
1 lettuce
2 large leaves fresh sorrel
3 oz (75 g) butter
1 lb (450 g) onions, chopped
salt
freshly ground black pepper
2 oz (50 g) flour
2 pints (1.2 litres) chicken stock
2 pints (1.2 litres) milk

Wash the spinach, lettuce and sorrel leaves. Drain well. Melt the butter in a large pan, add the onions, salt and pepper and cook for about 3 minutes until the onions begin to soften. Add the spinach, lettuce and sorrel leaves and cook for a further 2 minutes. Add the flour, stir well and cook for a minute. Gradually blend in the stock, stirring until thickened. Simmer gently for about 10 minutes until the leaves are tender. Remove from the heat and leave to cool. Reduce to a purée in a processor or blender. Rinse out the saucepan, return the purée to the pan and bring back to the boil. Stir in the milk and heat until piping hot. Taste and check seasoning before serving in a tureen.

Serves 10-12

Five Bean Salad

It is essential to soak the dried beans overnight and also to cook the beans separately as the cooking times are all different. Also in the case of the aduki beans and red kidney beans the colour comes out and will discolour the white haricot and green flageolet beans if they are cooked together.

8 oz (225 g) flageolet beans
8 oz (225 g) red kidney beans
8 oz (225 g) aduki beans
8 oz (225 g) haricot beans
8 oz (225 g) cooked small broad
  beans
1 fat clove garlic, crushed
a small head of celery, chopped
1 small onion, chopped
about 8 tablespoons French
  dressing
chopped parsley to garnish

Soak the uncooked beans overnight in cold water. Drain well and cook separately according to the instructions on the side of the packets. Rinse under hot water while still warm, put in a bowl and toss with the other ingredients. Leave in a cool place to marinate overnight.

Turn into a serving dish and sprinkle with parsley just before serving.

Serves 10-15 with other salads

Green Salad

1 Cos lettuce
1 Webbs lettuce
about ½ curly endive, or 2 heads
  chicory
½ cucumber
1 small green pepper
8 tablespoons French dressing
3 spring onions
½ bunch watercress
2 tablespoons sunflower seeds

Wash the lettuces, drain and tear into small pieces. Shred the endive coarsely or break the leaves off the chicory. Dice the cucumber. De-seed and remove the pith from the pepper and slice. Put the French dressing in a bowl with the chopped spring onions, arrange the lettuce, endive, pepper and cucumber on top, then add the watercress. Sprinkle with sunflower seeds, toss just before serving.

Serves 10

Old-fashioned Ox Tongue

Remember to order the ox tongue well in advance from the butcher as he will need to salt it in brine for you. When serving it on the buffet table, be sure it is well chilled so that it will slice easily.

1 salted ox tongue
2 bay leaves
1 medium onion, roughly chopped
6 peppercorns
watercress to garnish

Put the ox tongue in a pan just large enough to take the tongue, with the bay leaves, onion and peppercorns. Add sufficient water just to cover the tongue. Bring to the boil, cover with a lid and simmer gently for about 4 hours until tender. Lift the tongue out of the liquor and cool until cool enough to handle. Remove the skin and any fat and small bones from the top of the tongue. Put the tongue down flat on a board and cut through it lengthways, so it is split in half. Curl one piece of tongue up and put cut side down in a 6 inch (15 cm) cake tin or small pan. Put the other half of the tongue on top, cut side uppermost, place a small flat plate or saucer on top and weigh down with weights until the juices from the tongue come up level with the container.

Refrigerate overnight before turning the tongue out. To turn out, dip the tin or pan in a bowl of boiling water for a few moments, then turn out onto a plate and serve garnished with watercress.

Serve 15 with other meats

Hors d'Oeuvre

This recipe can be used as a starter or I sometimes increase the portions and serve it as a light lunch with crusty French bread.

10 small eggs, size 6
2 oz (56 g) can anchovy fillets in oil, drained
1 lb (450 g) peeled prawns
a few sprigs fresh dill
2 bunches watercress, stalks and tatty leaves removed

For the mayonnaise
1 egg
½ teaspoon salt
plenty of freshly ground black pepper
½ teaspoon made mustard
½ teaspoon caster sugar
1 dessertspoon white wine vinegar
½ pint (300 ml) sunflower oil
juice of ½ lemon

For the herring mixture
2 × 8 oz (250 g) jars marina herring fillets in wine sauce

Hors d'Oeuvre

juice of 1 lemon
5 fl oz (142 ml) carton soured cream
½ teaspoon turmeric
2 small red dessert apples, cored and sliced

For the mushroom salad
¼ pint (150 ml) water
4 tablespoons sunflower oil
salt
freshly ground black pepper
½ teaspoon ground coriander
12 oz (350 g) small button mushrooms
4 fl oz (100 ml) Madeira
2 sticks celery, sliced

For the French dressing
½ teaspoon dry mustard
1 dessertspoon caster sugar
4 tablespoons white wine vinegar
8 tablespoons sunflower oil
salt
freshly ground black pepper

For the carrot salad
4 large carrots
juice of 1 lemon

salt
freshly ground black pepper

For the red cabbage salad
12 oz (350 g) red cabbage, finely shredded
6 spring onions, chopped
1 teaspoon fennel or dill seed
½ recipe for French dressing (above)
salt
freshly ground black pepper

For the lettuce salad
1 small iceberg lettuce, finely shredded
2 tablespoons freshly chopped parsley
½ recipe for French dressing (above)
salt
freshly ground black pepper

Preparation the day before

Hard-boil the eggs for about 10 minutes in a pan of simmering water. Cool quickly under running cold water to prevent a dark ring from forming around the yolk.

Prepare the mayonnaise. Put all the ingredients except the oil and lemon juice in a processor or blender and process for a few moments, then add the oil in a slow steady stream until all has been added. The mayonnaise will now be thick. Add the lemon juice and process again. Taste and check seasoning, store in the refrigerator.

For the herring mixture, drain the liquid from the herrings, slice the herring fillets into long strips, put in a bowl with the remaining ingredients, except the apple, mix well and store in the refrigerator.

Prepare the mushroom salad. Put the water, oil, seasoning, coriander and whole mushrooms in a pan. Bring to the boil, simmer gently without a lid for about 5 minutes, lift out the mushrooms with a slotted spoon into a bowl. Add the Madeira to the liquid left in the pan, boil rapidly until reduced to a syrup, then pour over the mushrooms. Cool and refrigerate until required.

For the French dressing, mix the mustard, sugar and vinegar together, stir in the oil and seasoning. Store in the refrigerator.

Preparation on the day

Prepare the carrot salad. Grate the carrots and toss in lemon juice. Season well with salt and pepper.

Add the celery to the mushroom mixture.

Stir the apple into the herring mixture.

Prepare the red cabbage salad. Mix all the ingredients together in a bowl until thoroughly coated in the dressing.

Prepare the lettuce salad. Combine all the ingredients together in a bowl.

To assemble the hors d'oeuvre

Using the photograph as a guide, assemble the hors d'oeuvre on individual plates. Put 1 egg on the side of each plate, coat with mayonnaise and garnish with a rolled up anchovy fillet. Put a portion of prawns next to the egg and garnish with a sprig of dill. Next put a portion of lettuce salad, then red cabbage and continue around the plate ending with a bunch of watercress.

Serves 10

All-the-year-round Simnel Cake

This is traditionally an Easter cake but we love it at any time of the year.

6 oz (175 g) soft margarine
6 oz (175 g) light muscovado sugar
3 eggs
6 oz (175 g) plain flour
3 level teaspoons mixed spice
1 level teaspoon baking powder
2 tablespoons milk
10 oz (275 g) mixed dried fruit
2 oz (50 g) glacé cherries
finely grated rind of 1 lemon
2 oz (50 g) ground almonds
8 oz (225 g) almond paste
½ oz (12.5 g) flaked almonds

Heat the oven to 325°F/160°C/gas mark 3. Grease and line with greased greaseproof paper a 7 inch (17.5 cm) round cake tin.

Put all the ingredients for the cake in a mixing bowl and beat well for about 2 minutes until well blended. Place half the mixture in the bottom of the tin and smooth the top. Take the almond paste and roll out to a circle the size of the tin and put on top of the cake mixture. Cover with the remaining cake mixture, smooth the top and sprinkle with the flaked almonds. Bake in the oven for about 2¼ hours or until a skewer comes out clean when pierced into the centre of the cake. Turn out, remove the paper and leave to cool on a wire rack.

Chicken and Tarragon Raised Pie

The pastry for this pie is very easy to make and is lovely and crisp. It is a nice change from the more usual shortcrust.

Filling
3½ lb (1.5 kg) chicken
8 oz (225 g) pork sausagemeat
1 tablespoon fresh tarragon, chopped
1 teaspoon ground mace
2 teaspoons salt
freshly ground black pepper
8 oz (225 g) piece of ham, cut into long thin strips
6 small hard-boiled eggs, shelled with the white trimmed from each end so that the yolk is just showing through
beaten egg and milk to glaze

Pastry
12 oz (350 g) plain flour
1 teaspoon salt
5 oz (150 g) lard
¼ pint (150 ml) plus 2 tablespoons water

Grease a 2 lb (1.2 kg) loaf tin.

First carve off the legs and thighs from the raw chicken, then remove the skin and bones. Take the meat off the rest of the bird, discard the skin and make stock from all the bones. Cube all the chicken and put in a bowl with the sausagemeat, tarragon, mace and seasonings.

Now make the pastry. Put the flour and salt in a bowl. Place the lard and water in a pan and allow the water to boil and the lard to melt. Make a well in the centre of the flour and pour in all the liquid, mixing quickly with a wooden spoon until it becomes a smooth dough. When cool enough to handle, take two-thirds of the dough and work it round the inside and up the sides of the tin. Arrange half the strips of ham in the bottom of the tin, followed by half the meat mixture. Make six dents in the mixture and arrange the eggs end to end along the length of the tin. Cover with the remaining meat mixture and the strips of ham. Knead the remaining one-third of pastry into an oblong big enough to cover the top of the pie, press the edges firmly together and flute or just press with the prongs of a fork. Make four small holes in the top of the pie and decorate with pastry leaves if liked. Brush with beaten egg and milk and cook in the oven at 425°/220°C/gas mark 7 for 45 minutes, then reduce the heat to 350°F/180°C/gas mark 4 for a further 30 minutes. Remove from the oven and leave to cool in the tin. Chill the pie overnight before turning out and serving whole on a plate garnished with salad, or you might like to cut it in slices before arranging on a serving plate.

Serves 10

Chicken and Tarragon Raised Pie

CHILDREN'S BIRTHDAY PARTY

The type of party depends so much on the age of the child.
The very young usually enjoy games, a traditional tea with all
the things they like, and a few novel ideas, such as tiny iced buns
with their names on, individual brightly-coloured, animal-
moulded jellies, and funny wiggly-shaped straws for their drinks.
The 8-13-year-olds might well go for a barbecue in summer or a
lunch outside. Instead of making a cake, serve a baked alaska
pudding smothered in those long thin candles. Another
idea that my own children enjoy is a pizza party; all different
kinds of pizzas followed by ice cream served in sundae glasses
with all sorts of fruit sauces and cream – a glorified knickerbocker glory.
The over-13s still enjoy a barbecue with all the usual
favourites, or maybe an outing followed by a special supper at home.

Pizza Party

This is enough for 10 hungry adults and children. Make up the dough with a 1½ lb (675 g) packet of bread mix, either brown or white. This will give three 9 inch (22.5 cm) bases.

Dough
1½ lb (675 g) packet bread mix, either brown or white

General tomato base
2 tablespoons sunflower oil
3 large onions, chopped
3 × 14 oz (397 g) cans tomatoes
14 oz (397 g) can tomato purée
3 cloves garlic, crushed
2 teaspoons sugar
salt
freshly ground black pepper
a few mixed herbs, chopped

Bacon and mushroom topping
3 tablespoons sunflower oil
8 oz (225 g) button mushrooms, sliced
16 thin rashers streaky bacon

Sausage topping
1 lb (450 g) pork sausagemeat

Cheese, tomato and green pepper topping
6 oz (175 g) Cheddar cheese, grated
1 small green pepper, seeded and chopped
salt
freshly ground black pepper

First make up the dough according to the instructions on the packet.

For the general tomato base, heat the oil in a pan, add the onions and fry until soft. Add the remaining ingredients and cook without a lid until the mixture is thick and pulpy. Taste and check seasoning – if liked, add a few chopped herbs.

For the bacon and mushroom topping, measure the oil into a pan and fry the mushrooms quickly for 1 minute. Remove the rind from the bacon.

For the sausage topping, flatten the sausagemeat in a large nonstick pan to about 9 inches (22.5 cm) in diameter to form a cake. Fry on both sides until browned and cooked through, this will take about 10 minutes.

To assemble, divide the dough into three equal pieces, flatten out each piece on lightly floured baking trays to 9 inch (22.5 cm) circles. Brush each pizza with oil and spread with the general tomato base. Now cover each with the toppings.

Bacon and mushroom topping: spread over the mushrooms and arrange the bacon on top to give a cartwheel effect.
Sausage topping: lift the sausagemeat cake on top of the pizza.
Cheese, tomato and green pepper topping: scatter the cheese and green pepper on the pizza and season.

Bake at 425°F/220°C/gas mark 7 for about 20 minutes, then lower the heat to 375°F/190°C/gas mark 5 for a further 20 minutes, or until the pizzas are evenly cooked and pale brown at the edges. Serve hot with a mixed salad.

Serves 10

Muffin Pizzas

Children in particular simply adore these mini pizzas; they are ideal to serve at a party as they don't necessarily have to be eaten with a knife and fork.

6 muffins
1 oz (25 g) butter
8 oz (225 g) onions, chopped
8 oz (225 g) can tomatoes
½ teaspoon mixed dried herbs
freshly ground black pepper
salt
6 oz (175 g) mature Cheddar cheese, grated
2 oz (50 g) anchovy fillets, drained

Melt the butter in a pan and fry the onions for about 5 minutes until beginning to soften. Add the contents of the can of tomatoes and continue to cook for about a further 5 minutes until the mixture has reduced to a thick pulp. Add the herbs and season.

Slice the muffins in half and divide the tomato mixture between them, spreading it out evenly over the tops of the muffins. Sprinkle with cheese and arrange the anchovy fillets on top. Heat the grill, lift the pizzas on to the grill pan and grill for about 8 minutes until the cheese has melted and is bubbling.

Makes 12 pizzas

Chicken Kebabs

These can be prepared well ahead and kept in the refrigerator until required. The marinade makes them that bit more special. Either cook on a barbecue or under a grill.

4 chicken breasts, with skin and bone removed

For the marinade
8 tablespoons sunflower oil
3 fat cloves garlic, crushed
2 tablespoons white wine vinegar
1 medium onion, chopped

Vegetables
4 small onions, cut into quarters
8 oz (225 g) button mushrooms
1 red pepper, seeded and cut into 1 inch (2.5 cm) pieces
1 green pepper, seeded and cut into 1 inch (2.5 cm) pieces
salt and freshly ground black pepper

Cut the chicken breasts into neat, bite-size chunks. Put into a bowl with the ingredients for the marinade and mix well. Cover with cling film and chill in the refrigerator overnight.

The next day, lift the chicken out of the marinade and arrange on 8 flat skewers with the wedges of onion, mushrooms and pieces of pepper. Brush the kebabs with the marinade, season well and cook on a barbecue or under a hot grill for 10-15 minutes until the chicken is cooked. Be sure to keep brushing the kebabs with the marinade and turning them during cooking. Arrange in a dish and serve with a green salad tossed in French dressing.

Serves 8

Home-made Beefburgers

These are so much nicer than the commercially bought ones and really are so simple to prepare. Make sure that the mixture is really well chilled before cooking them.

12 oz (350 g) raw minced beef
2 oz (50 g) butter
8 oz (225 g) onions, chopped
2 oz (50 g) fresh brown breadcrumbs
1 egg, beaten
2 tablespoons freshly chopped parsley
salt
freshly ground black pepper

Heat the butter in a pan and quickly fry the onions for about 5 minutes until beginning to soften. Put the onions in a bowl, add the minced beef, breadcrumbs, egg and parsley and season well. Mix well until the mixture is thoroughly blended. Divide the mixture into eight. With lightly floured hands shape the mixture into balls and flatten to form a 'burger'. Chill in the refrigerator for about 5 hours before cooking.

To cook, heat the grill and cook the burgers for about 15 minutes until cooked through, turning once during cooking. Serve in bread buns with relish.

Makes 8 burgers

Special Barbecue Chicken

This glaze gives the chicken an absolutely delicious flavour; it is well worth coating the portions before cooking them.

6 chicken portions
salt
freshly ground black pepper

For the glaze
2 tablespoons tomato ketchup
2 tablespoons sunflower oil
2 tablespoons dark muscovado sugar
2 tablespoons white wine vinegar

Heat the oven to 425°F/220°C/gas mark 7.

Put all the ingredients for the glaze in a bowl and mix well until blended to give a runny syrup.

Arrange the portions in a roasting tin and season well with salt and pepper. Brush with the glaze so that they are evenly coated and cook in the oven for about 40 minutes until tender. Keep basting the chicken portions with the glaze during cooking. To test when the chicken is cooked, pierce the thickest part with a skewer; if the juices that run out are clear, the chicken is cooked.

Serves 6

Smartie Cakes

Make these in sweet paper cases. Young children love them because they are so small; they can eat five or six. I find a large cupcake overwhelms them sometimes.

about 50 sweet paper cases
4 oz (100 g) soft margarine
2 eggs
4 oz (100 g) self-raising flour
1 level teaspoon baking powder
4 oz (100 g) caster sugar

To decorate
4 oz (100 g) icing sugar, sieved
about 1 tablespoon lemon juice
about 50 Smarties

Heat the oven to 350°F/180°C/gas mark 4. Arrange sweet paper cases on a baking tray.

Put the margarine, eggs, flour, baking powder and sugar together in a bowl and beat well for about 2 minutes until well blended. Divide the mixture between the paper cases. Bake in the oven for about 12-15 minutes until pale golden brown. Cool on a wire rack. Make the glacé icing by mixing the icing sugar and lemon juice to a spreading consistency. Spread a little on the top of each cake with a small palette knife and decorate with a Smartie, once the icing is almost set, otherwise the colour will run from the sweet.

Makes about 50 cakes

Shaped Biscuits

Use as many different shaped cutters
as you have to give a good assortment
of biscuits.

8 oz (225 g) plain flour
4 oz (100 g) butter
4 oz (100 g) caster sugar
1 egg, lightly beaten

To decorate
4 oz (100 g) plain chocolate, melted

Heat the oven to 350°F/180°C/gas
mark 4. Lightly grease two large baking trays. Measure the flour into a
bowl and rub in the butter until the
mixture resembles fine breadcrumbs,
stir in the sugar and bind the mixture
together with the egg to form a stiff
dough. Wrap in cling film and chill in
the refrigerator for 15 minutes. Turn
the dough out onto a lightly floured
surface, knead until smooth, then
roll out to ¼ inch (7 mm) thick. Cut
out biscuits with different shaped cutters, lift onto the baking tray and
cook for about 12 minutes in the oven
until a straw colour. Lift onto a wire
rack with a palette knife to cool.

To decorate biscuits, dip them in
melted chocolate so that they are half
coated. Leave to set in a cool place on
silicone paper.

Makes about 30 biscuits depending
on size

Smartie Cakes (see page 53) *and Shaped Biscuits*

Baked Alaska

Baked Alaska

Serve this at a children's birthday
party instead of the usual birthday
cake. You can put long thin candles
on top which look fun, or decorate
with a sparkler.

1 raspberry-filled swiss roll
a small block of the children's
favourite ice cream
2 egg whites
4 oz (100 g) caster sugar

Cut the swiss roll into 8 slices, arrange
these on an ovenproof serving plate
so that they touch. Arrange slices of
ice cream on top of the sponge, then
make the meringue topping. Whisk
the egg whites with an electric whisk
until beginning to form peaks, whisk
in the sugar a teaspoonful at a time,
beating for about 5 minutes. Spoon
meringue over the ice cream so that
the ice cream is sealed inside. Store in
the freezer until required, then cook
in the oven at 425°F/220°C/gas
mark 7 for about 3 minutes until the

meringue is beginning to turn a
golden brown. Take out of oven, put
in candles and serve immediately.

Serves 6-8

PUDDINGS

The celebration puddings here can all be made in advance.
Before you begin, however, make sure you have suitable
dishes to make and serve them in. If you have one beautiful glass
bowl, use it perhaps for a mousse, or strawberries and peaches
in orange juice, or piled with scoopfuls of ice cream or
sorbet. If you don't have enough ramekins or small *pot au chocolat*
pots for individual mousses or other puddings, use wine glasses.
One of the simplest ideas is to take a large oval meat plate
and (for 10 people) have a melon, mango, pawpaw,
two kiwi fruit, some large grapes and a punnet of
strawberries. Slice the fruit, removing the peel and the pips of
the first three. Peel and slice the kiwi and pineapple,
saving the top of the pineapple. Arrange the sliced fruit,
grapes and strawberries on the meat plate and place the pineapple
top at the end. Cover with cling film and chill for 1 hour. This
looks fantastic and is so easy. Everyone can help
themselves and there is no need for cream and sugar.

Lemon Cream Sorbet and Orange Cream Sorbet

These two ice creams are a cross between a sorbet and an ice cream. There is no need for an ice cream machine as a processor works well for this recipe. I have always had difficulty in the past freezing the sorbets until they were slushy, as it meant continuously checking the freezer. With this recipe, freeze the sorbet until it is firm, process and then refreeze. Serve in scoopfuls straight from the freezer; it will not be too hard to do this.

For the Lemon Cream Sorbet
½ pint (300 ml) double cream
grated rind and juice of 2 lemons
12 oz (350 g) caster sugar
1 pint (600 ml) milk

For the Orange Cream Sorbet
½ pint (300 ml) double cream, whipped
6 fl oz (175 ml) frozen concentrated orange juice, thawed
12 oz (350 g) caster sugar
1 pint (600 ml) milk

Lemon Cream Sorbet and Strawberries and Peaches in Orange Juice

Pour the cream into a large mixing bowl, whisk until it forms stiff peaks, then stir in the lemon rind and juice, sugar and milk until evenly blended. Pour into a 2 pint (1.2 litre) container and cover with a lid. Freeze until firm, cut into cubes and process until smooth and creamy. Return to the container and freeze until required.

To make the orange cream sorbet, follow the method for lemon cream sorbet but add the orange juice in place of the lemon rind and juice.

To make cream sorbets without a processor, freeze until thick and soft, whisk with an electric whisk until smooth and creamy, then refreeze.

Serves 10-12

Strawberries and Peaches in Orange Juice

A simple refreshing dessert.

4 fresh peaches
juice of 1 orange
1 lb (450 g) small strawberries
3 oz (75 g) caster sugar

Cut the peaches in half and remove the stones. Peel, slice into the bottom of a glass serving dish and cover immediately with the orange juice. Hull and slice the strawberries and arrange on top of the peaches. Sprinkle with the caster sugar, cover with cling film and chill in the refrigerator for several hours before serving. To serve, gently mix the two fruits so that they are evenly blended.

Serves 8

Religieuses

These make a super change from the usual profiteroles or eclairs. Make the choux pastry ahead, then fill just before they are required, so that the pastry remains nice and crisp.

Choux pastry
2 oz (50 g) butter
¼ pint (150 ml) water
2½ oz (62.5 g) plain flour
2 eggs, beaten

Filling
½ pint (300 ml) whipping cream, whipped
4 teaspoons coffee essence
1 oz (25 g) icing sugar, sieved

Icing
1½ oz (40 g) butter
1 oz (25 g) cocoa, sieved
4 oz (100 g) icing sugar, sieved
3 tablespoons milk

Heat the oven to 425°F/220°C/gas mark 7. Prepare the choux pastry in the usual way (see Baby Cheese Eclairs, page 21). Put the mixture in a piping bag fitted with a ½ inch (1.25 cm) plain icing nozzle, pipe into 10 small and 10 slightly larger blobs on a lightly greased baking tray. Cook in the oven for 10 minutes, reduce the temperature to 375°F/190°C/gas mark 5 and cook for a further 20 minutes until well risen and golden brown. Remove from the oven and split one side of each bun to allow the steam to escape. Cool on a wire rack.

Put about 3 tablespoons of the whipping cream to one side. Mix the remainder with the coffee essence and icing sugar. Spoon this into the middle of the buns.

For the icing, melt the butter in a small pan and stir in the cocoa, cook gently for a minute. Remove from the heat and stir in the icing sugar and milk, beat well until starting to thicken. Dip each bun in the icing to cover the top, stand a small bun on top of each of the larger buns. Put the reserved cream in a piping bag fitted with a small star-shaped nozzle, pipe rosettes around the religieuses where the two buns join. Serve on the same day as they are made.

Makes about 10 religieuses

Religieuses

Tropical Pavlova

Vary the fruit with whatever unusual fruit you can get hold of.

3 egg whites
6 oz (175 g) caster sugar
2 passion fruit
½ pint (300 ml) whipping cream, whipped
2 kiwi fruit
1 mango
a little caster sugar to sweeten

Lay a sheet of silicone paper on a baking tray and mark an 8 inch (20 cm) circle on it. Heat the oven to 325°F/160°C/gas mark 3.

Whisk the egg whites with an electric whisk until stiff and add the sugar a teaspoonful at a time. Spread the meringue out to cover the circle on the baking tray, building up the sides so they are higher than the middle.

Reduce the oven temperature to 300°F/150°C/gas mark 2 and bake for about an hour. Turn the oven off and

let the pavlova become quite cold in the oven. Remove from the baking tray and put on a serving plate.

Cut the passion fruit in half, scoop out the flesh and seeds and stir into the whipped cream. Peel the kiwi fruit and cut in slices, peel and slice the mango, save a few slices of each for decoration and stir the remainder into the cream. Taste and sweeten as required. Pile the cream mixture into the pavlova and decorate.

Serves 6-8

Four Seasons Fresh Fruit Sponge Cake

I have called this four seasons as you can substitute different fillings depending on the time of year.

For the sponge
6 eggs
6 oz (175 g) caster sugar, warmed
6 oz (175 g) self-raising flour

For the filling
pineapple jam
1 whole small fresh pineapple with skin and core removed, chopped
½ pint (300 ml) whipping cream, whipped

To decorate
a little sieved icing sugar
a sprig of fresh mint or lemon balm

Heat the oven to 350°F/180°C/gas mark 4. Grease a 10 inch (25 cm) deep round cake tin and line with a circle of greased greaseproof paper.

Pour nearly boiling water into the mixing bowl with the beaters in, then pour away the water; this heats both the bowl and the beaters. Break the eggs into the heated bowl and whisk in the sugar until the mixture is light and creamy and will leave a trail when the whisk is lifted out. Carefully fold in the flour until evenly blended.

Pour the mixture into the lined tin and bake in the oven for about 35 minutes until the top of the cake springs back when lightly pressed with a finger. Turn out and leave to cool on a wire rack.

Split the sponge in half and spread both halves with the jam, mix the pineapple and cream together and use to sandwich the two halves together. Lift onto a serving plate, then dredge with a little icing sugar to serve, and decorate with a sprig of fresh mint or lemon balm.

Serves 10

Four Seasons Fresh Fruit Sponge Cake

Refreshing Lemon Mousse

This is a very refreshing mousse, which is ideal after a large meal.

8 eggs
8 oz (225 g) caster sugar
4 large lemons
1 oz (25 g) powdered gelatine
6 tablespoons cold water
whipped cream and lemon slices and mint to decorate

Separate the eggs, put the yolks in a bowl with the sugar and beat until well blended and creamy. Put the whites in a separate bowl ready for whisking.

Grate the rind and squeeze the juice from the lemons and add both to the yolk mixture. Put the gelatine and water in a small bowl and leave for about 3 minutes to form a sponge. Allow the gelatine to dissolve over a pan of simmering water, cool slightly and stir into the yolk mixture. Leave to cool but not set.

Whisk the egg whites, using an electric hand whisk until stiff, then fold into the lemon mixture. Pour into two 2 pint (1.2 litre) glass dishes or, if you have one, one large 4 pint (2.4 litre) dish and chill in the refrigerator for at least 4 hours until set. Decorate with whipped cream and lemon slices and mint.

Serves 10

QUANTITIES

Food for a crowd

It is difficult to give exact quantities that people are going to eat; a lot depends on the age of the guests (16-20-year-olds often have wonderful appetites!). The time of day is important too: if it is a long time since the previous meal, they could be ravenous; other times they may not be so hungry. For instance, I find that the day after Boxing Day, which is usually a holiday, appetites can be rather jaded after all the feasting over Christmas. However, the lists below are a general guide.

SANDWICHES
thin cut bread
1 large sandwich loaf contains about 24 slices
medium cut bread
1 large sandwich loaf contains about 20 slices
thick cut bread
1 large sandwich loaf contains about 16 slices
French bread
1 long stick cuts into about 20 slices
butter
1 lb (450 g) spreads about 4 medium cut loaves

6 chopped hard-boiled eggs mixed with mayonnaise fill about 12 rounds of sandwiches
3 × 7¾ oz (200 g) cans salmon, flaked and mixed with mayonnaise, fill about 12 rounds of sandwiches

LIQUIDS
milk for tea
1 pint (600 ml) is enough for 20 cups
milk for coffee
1 pint (600 ml) is enough for 20 cups (less if the milk is hot)

single cream for coffee
1 pint (600 ml) is enough for 20 cups
single cream for fruit salad, etc.
1 pint (600 ml) is enough for about 12 portions
double cream for fruit salad, etc.
1 pint (600 ml) is enough for 12-15 portions

SAVOURY DISHES
salted nuts
½ oz (12.5 g) per person
potato crisps
1 oz (25 g) per person
meat for casserole
6 oz (175 g) per person
joint with bone
6-8 oz (175-225 g) per person
joint without bone
4-6 oz (100-175 g) per person
steak
6 oz (175 g) per person
salmon
4-5 oz (100-125 g) per person
rice
1½-2 oz (40-50 g) uncooked rice per person
pasta
3-4 oz (75-100 g) uncooked pasta per person
soup
1 pint (600 ml) will serve 3 people
sauce
½ pint (300 ml) will serve 4 people

DESSERTS
strawberries
4 oz (100 g) per person
raspberries
3-4 oz (75-100 g) per person
fruit salad
2 pints (1.2 litres) will serve 8 people
meringues
6 egg whites, 12 oz (350 g) caster sugar makes about 30 small meringue pairs
cakes
a 10 inch (25 cm) sponge will serve 16 people

Amount of food per person at parties

Drinks party
6-8 savouries, 3-4 drinks
Finger buffet
7 savouries, 3 sweet items (e.g. meringues, eclairs, 1 piece cake), 3-4 drinks
Fork buffet
1 first course, 1 main dish with accompaniments, 1 dessert or cheese, 3-4 drinks
Children's tea party
4-6 savouries, ice cream, 1 piece birthday cake, 1 other cake or biscuit, 2 cold drinks
Teenagers' party
1 main dish with accompaniments, 1 dessert, 3-4 drinks
Adults' tea party
4 small sandwiches, 2 cakes or pastries, 2 cups tea

DOING UP A VILLAGE HALL

A Wedding or Christening Party

When it comes to celebrating in style, don't let the splendour stop at the cake, the bride's trousseau or the floral displays. Use your imagination to transform the venue and make it a reception to remember.

The trick is to focus on the food and festivities and make sure the eye is taken away from everything else – the ceiling, shabby doors, a vast stage.

The stage

Start by surveying the stage, as this will take the most preparation. It is likely to need a focal point and mock columns in the corners will add to the sense of grandeur. They are easy to make from cardboard tubes, decorated with paint, fabric or paper. We covered ours with corrugated paper and painted them cream. You will probably need to use several strips (see the photograph at the front of the book). Look out for pieces used in packaging or buy a whole reel from a paper merchant (look in the Yellow Pages). When complete, add some trailing plants.

If you want to hide some of the stage, screens are ideal. Make them by nailing expanding trellis onto a wooden frame, then entwine with ribbons, and even add a few feathered birds for a hint of romance.

The windows

Lash out on lots of leafy plants and line along the sills (donate them to the couple's home afterwards). Alternatively, borrow some from green-fingered friends. If you have a pastel colour scheme like ours, you can use masses of garden twine to great effect. (Chukkatwine comes in orange, pink, lemon, and pink and blue, and is available from hardware shops.) Just cut long strips and let a bunch cascade from the sills, and even down the doors. Coloured netting looks good scrunched up behind the plants and at the same time gives some height and disguises the view. If the curtains

don't match your colour scheme, ask the caretaker if you can remove them for the day.

The walls

Another idea for keeping the emphasis at eye level is to run a frieze along the wall. You will need a long length of plain paper – lining paper (for walls) is ideal. Either paint a design freehand, or stencil; you can buy stencil designs in good art and book shops. Alternatively, buy some waxed paper and cut your own design. It is tricky to cut out – you will need to press down hard with a modelling knife or scalpel – so it is best to do a little at a time. For perfect results, you need to apply the paint with a stencil brush, but this would take forever, so use sprays instead; the finish will be a little smudgy but effective.

Start by measuring the walls. If they are broken up by a pillar or door, decide how many designs should be between each, then mark on the paper where the motifs should be. Again it is easier to work in panels, preferably in a garage or workroom. Tape the stencil down to the paper using masking tape and, if it lifts from the surface, use dressmaking pins horizontally to prevent the paint from creeping underneath. As more paint is applied, it will get heavier and will not lift as much. When spraying, be sure that the room is well ventilated. Glue wide ribbon along the top and bottom of the frieze.

The doors

Add lining paper panels and bunches of Chukkatwine but take care not to obstruct entrances.

The tables

The answer to covering so many tables while keeping the cost down is to invest in a giant banqueting roll. It comes in bulk and is available from catering suppliers. (Derry by *Deeko* is the nicest and most expensive, but they do stock a range of designs.)

Add some glamour to the buffet table and/or top table with flounces of fabric threaded through hoops. To make satin-covered hoops, you will

need large (90 mm diameter) wooden curtain rings. Wind 24 inches (60 cm) of 1 inch (2.5 cm) wide ribbon around each ring, starting and finishing at the same place. Decorate by twisting wired fabric flowers around. Knock a tack through the eyelet of the hoop into the edge of the table, spacing rings equally. You will need about double the length of the table of fabric to loop through the hoops. By using two different types of fabric you get a contrast in texture and keep the cost down – we used soft sheer voile and scrunchy netting.

Place settings

You will need a team of helpers for these, unless you start well in advance and do them gradually. Make bow ties for the men, fans for the women, each bearing the name of the guest. Make a fan by pleating coloured paper and glue lace along the edge. To make it stand up, you'll need to make a base. Glue each pleat together along the base, cut as shown and bend the longer pieces outwards. Tie a ribbon around the bottom and slot in a name card. To make a bow tie, cut a strip of fabric 15 x 6 inches (38 x 15 cm) and fold as shown. Wind a smaller piece of fabric 7½ x 5 inches (19 x 14 cm) around the centre of the large piece and glue. Fold the name card as shown and glue on the bow tie.

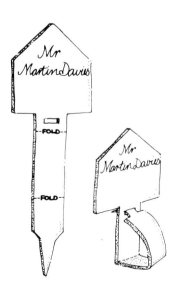

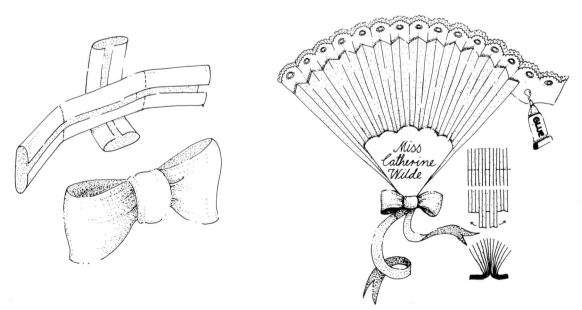

Children's Jungle Party

To make sure the party is an all-round success, it is worth spending some time setting the scene. We recruited a crew of helpers and started preparations with a 'paint-in' in the garage where family and friends contributed to a mammoth collage and the Dads were persuaded to knock up a jungle hut roof from timber and straw to stand over the serving table. Here are some of our ideas to set you thinking.

The collage

This is a giant frieze (part painted, part fabric scraps and odds and ends) which will decorate the walls of the hall. The best backing paper to use is Anaglypta wallpaper. It is cheap and its knobbly texture looks like jungly ferns and bushes once painted. Use up old tins of paint or look for reduced discontinued shades of greens and browns in the shops – just slosh it on Rolf Harris style in blocks for bushes and streaks to suggest grasses. Work in panels; vertical for trees, horizontal for undergrowth. This way it is easy to transport and you just build up the scene when you get to the hall – don't forget to measure the walls before you start though. Crinkle up plain brown paper for tree trunks, or better still use corrugated paper – the flutes make convincing bark. Make a palm tree by cutting out triangles of corrugated paper and paste onto the background with gaps between them. Cut massive leaves from green plastic sacks (the best kind are those that hold animal feed or fertiliser as they are very tough – ours came from a farm). Finish off with coconuts made from blown-up balloons with tufts of raffia.

No jungle is complete without its birds and beasts. Make them from scraps of fabric or paper. Use colourful illustrations in children's books for inspiration. Try converting a feather duster into a jolly parrot. First cut the shape from card, then glue on feathers using red for the head and body, blue and yellow for the tail. Make a beak from black paper. Colour pipe cleaners black with a felt pen, twist together

and bend into shape to form a claw. Add an eye . . . we bought two plastic ones from a toy making department of a store. Make a toucan by mounting tissue paper on card. Terylene wadding (the kind used for quilting) makes a perfect lion's mane. Colour it vibrant orange using poster paint, then pull to fluff it out. Cut eyes, nose and ears from felt scraps, and whiskers from snippets of wool.

If you can't cope with making complete animals, stick to parts: a lofty giraffe's neck from brown paper with yellow spots (a plastic carrier bag); a droopy elephants's trunk from grey tissue paper or interfacing. Make up black and white stripes from paper or fabric to suggest a zebra in the jungle, or orange and white to hint at a tiger lurking in the long grass.

On the table

Get the cheapest white paper table-cloths you can find and add your own decorations. Try painting a long grass border around the edge or cut out giant pawprints from black paper and make a trail up the walls and over the floor and table. Launch a 'Hunt the bear' competition and award a prize to the child who tracks down the end of the trail. Alternatively, choose a brightly-coloured party table cover to match cheerful disposable tableware. We found some wonderful animal designs by *Partyhouse* including invitations, loot bags and place setting cards. Or make your own place setting cards with animal facts on them.

The serving table/bar

It is best to convert this into a jungle hut. You can do this by making a roof from straw. (Ask at a farm or good pet shop.)

Start with a large piece of cardboard. Large boxes are ideal; they're often discarded by electrical shops, factories, cycle shops, etc. Bind bunches of straw with tape, then stick down each bundle individually on the card, working in rows. It is best to get a team together to do this and be prepared for a mess – the straw gets everywhere. In its simplest form set over a small table, you may get away

with using a folded piece of card and suspending it over a line between two wooden uprights. Fold the card before you start in this case. Or use two sides of a box like a hinge. For a sturdier structure, make a proper framework from wood or use one sheet of card and simply attach to four uprights. Insert each upright in a bucket of sand and stand on the table top.

Raid the garden shed – you will be surprised at how many jungly bits and pieces you find, such as a garden net which you can thread with twigs to give a forest effect.

The finishing touches

Ask all the guests to bring along something to add to the atmosphere. The children can bring a favourite toy animal. If you want to buy some, there is a marvellous mail order company called Curious Caterpillar by Post that has a catalogue of novelties including creepy crawlies and masses of other small gifts that make ideal prizes or presents to take home. Ask the mums to donate a plant for the day – anything from scrawny spider plants, which look like jungle grasses, to outsize rubber trees. Shine lamps through the leaves to create larger-than-life shadows.

Last but not least, check the rules with the caretaker.

● Find out what you can and can't put on the walls to attach your decorations. (Sticky tape can cause paint to peel off when you remove it and may not be strong enough to hold your decorations. Blu-tac and masking tape are better and usually more acceptable.) You will probably find hooks and nails in the walls already.

● Ask what there will be at your disposal. (You will probably find a spare balloon net somewhere, some trestle tables and even some china.)

● Overbook your time; you will probably need at least a morning to set the place up.

● And most important, check fire regulations: you shouldn't obstruct fire doors at all and there are no doubt other regulations that will apply.

Useful addresses

Curious Caterpillar by Post, 102 Bancroft, Hitchin, Herts. Send a 9 x 6½ inch (23 x 16 cm) sae.

Deeko plc, Garman Road, London, N17 0UG.

Partyhouse. Stockists from Cloud 9, 199-205 Richmond Road, London, E8.

Woking Paper Tubes Company, Boundary Road, Woking, Surrey, GU21 5BX.

INDEX